Setting Boundaries

Set Everyday Boundaries for a Happy, Healthier You

Wilda Olsen

© **Copyright 2020 - All rights reserved.**

The content contained within this book may not be reproduced, duplicated, nor transmitted without direct written permission from the author or the publisher.

Under no circumstances will any blame or legal responsibility be held against the publisher, or author, for any damages, reparation, or monetary loss due to the information contained within this book, either directly or indirectly.

Legal Notice:

This book is copyright protected. It is only for personal use. You cannot amend, distribute, sell, use, quote or paraphrase any part, or the content within this book, without the consent of the author or publisher.

Disclaimer Notice:

Please note the information contained within this document is for educational and entertainment purposes only. All effort has been executed to present accurate, up to date, reliable, complete information. No warranties of any kind are declared or implied. Readers acknowledge that the author is not engaged in the rendering of legal, financial, medical, or professional advice. The content within this book has been derived from various sources. Please consult a licensed professional before attempting any techniques outlined in this book.

By reading this document, the reader agrees that under no circumstances is the author responsible for any losses, direct or indirect, that are incurred as a result of the use of the information contained within this document, including, but not limited to, errors, omissions, or inaccuracies.

Table of Contents

INTRODUCTION
- WHAT ARE BOUNDARIES?
- HOW THIS BOOK WILL BENEFIT YOU
- A BIT ABOUT THE AUTHOR

CHAPTER 1: ALL ABOUT BOUNDARIES
- WHY WE NEED BOUNDARIES
- A WORLD WITH NO BOUNDARIES
  - *Amy and Greg*
  - *Jane and Margaret*
  - *Joyce and Pamela*
- WHAT DOES SUCCESSFUL BOUNDARIES LOOK LIKE?
  - *Marissa and the Director*
  - *John*
- HOW TO RECOGNIZE THE NEED FOR BOUNDARIES

CHAPTER 2: GETTING STARTED WITH SETTING BOUNDARIES
- IDENTIFY AND UNDERSTAND YOUR CORE VALUES
- DECIDING THE RIGHT BOUNDARIES FOR YOU
  - *Boundaries Should Align to your Core Values*
  - *Know your Limits*
  - *Recognize Your Emotional Needs and Those of Others*
- MANAGING POTENTIAL INFRINGEMENTS TO YOUR BOUNDARIES

CHAPTER 3: BOUNDARIES FOR FRIENDS
- ALL FRIENDSHIPS REQUIRE BOUNDARIES
- HEALTHY FRIENDSHIPS REQUIRE CLEAR BOUNDARIES

    Communicate Clearly
    Allow Space Between You
    RESPECT EACH OTHER'S BELONGINGS
    IDENTIFYING DIFFERENT TYPES OF ABUSE
    LAST WORD

CHAPTER 4: BOUNDARIES FOR FAMILY

    THE INFLUENCES AT HOME
        Understanding the Relationship with your Parents
        Understanding the Relationship with your Siblings
        Understanding Extended Family
    MANAGING BOUNDARY VIOLATIONS FROM FAMILY
        Remain in Control
        Enacting Consequences
        Don't Take Their Reactions to Heart
        Seeking Support
    HEALTHY BOUNDARIES WITH YOUR PARTNER
        Identifying Toxic Boundaries
    HEALTHY BOUNDARIES FOR YOUR CHILDREN
    LAST WORD

CHAPTER 5: BOUNDARIES FOR WORK

    SUCCESSFUL PEOPLE SET BOUNDARIES
    WORKPLACE GUIDELINES TO CONSIDER
    COMMUNICATE YOUR CONCERNS
    SET STRUCTURE IN YOUR DAY
    KEEP YOUR PERSONAL LIFE SEPARATE
    KNOW YOUR COWORKERS AND THE RESOURCES AVAILABLE
    PREPARE FOR INFRINGEMENTS
    FINAL WORD

CHAPTER 6: BOUNDARIES FOR *YOU*

    ALL ABOUT SELF CARE
        Explore New Hobbies
        Guard Your Personal Boundaries

Janet
GIVE YOURSELF A BREAK
PHYSICAL BOUNDARIES TO ENSURE SELF-CARE
THE BENEFITS OF SELF-CARE AND STRESS MANAGEMENT
SELF-CARE TACTICS THAT REALLY WORK
NORMA

CHAPTER 7: MUTUAL GIVE AND TAKE

STEPS TO TAKE TOWARD BEING RESPECTFUL
Learning to Read Others
RECOGNIZING BOUNDARY VIOLATIONS
Trust in Your Intuition
Value Yourself
Respect the Other Person's Decision
Seek Permission
SUCCESSFUL WAYS IN WHICH TO SHOW RESPECT
Stay on the Alert
YOUR BOUNDARIES GROW WITH YOU
Understanding Your Past
Angela and Gary

A FINAL WORD

THE VALUE OF BOUNDARIES IN YOUR LIFE

RESOURCES

Introduction

Samantha's head snapped up from her desk where she had rested it briefly a moment before. The clanging of her cell phone jerked her alert. Her wary eyes stared at the screen where her boss' name was displayed. Now what?

Was her boss calling her to make changes to her proposal again for the umpteenth time today? Or was he phoning for an errand she needed to make first thing tomorrow morning?

Samantha now lived under constant stress from the unreasonable requests her boss was demanding of her. Even tonight, looking at the clock above her, her boss was calling her well past midnight when she should have already been asleep in bed.

The frustration and anxiety that she felt had her close to tears. She wasn't sure when it started being okay to be at her boss' beck and call, but it seems like any time her boss needed something, he had a free pass to her services. Samantha knew that she needed to put an end to this, but the idea of having to confront him was both too intimidating and overwhelming for her to even imagine.

You too might be feeling particularly vulnerable right now because you believe, and know, that people are abusing your goodwill, patience, your private space, as well as your peace.

So how do you extract yourself from this potentially destructive situation without hurting everyone's feelings? After all, you were possibly raised to believe everyone else's thoughts, feelings, and welfare comes before your own. If this is the case, it's now time to take a good, hard look at your own emotional, mental, and physical needs and decide how best to proceed with establishing the necessary boundaries, so that you can start protecting your own self-interests and well-being first.

What are Boundaries?

The term "boundary" may make you think of an enclosure or an expressly limited space, of being restricted or fenced in, or out, as the case may be. For the most part, boundaries are often viewed in a negative light. However, try seeing them as perimeters or borderlines that create no-go areas, actions and behaviors when dealing with others. These invisible lines take on a protective function that serves you and those around you. Setting boundaries often requires you to understand your needs, desires, fears and limits, so that you are able to protect yourself emotionally, physically, and mentally from unnecessary abuse.

Some psychologists will describe boundaries as those limits we set between ourselves and other people around us. Some of these borders are constructed during childhood - for example, when we are raised to be respectful of older members of our community and to address them politely, or to play fair at school and to share our resources. We learn quickly to treasure what is ours and to carefully guard certain items while willingly allowing our friends access to some of our belongings.

The challenge arises when our friends decide they have the right to more of our things than we feel comfortable sharing. Occasionally, situations of this nature can become volatile. And, unless we handle them immediately and put our boundaries in place, we are likely to discover people will continue to walk all over us, disregarding and disrespecting our personal space, our time and our items.

It can be challenging to stand up for yourself for fear of disappointing or angering others.

Sometimes, taking the path of least resistance seems the best option to keep the peace. But, have you ever considered the damage such action causes to *you*? Together, we can discover ways for you to overcome these types of situations to learn to grow your self-esteem and allow yourself the opportunity to flourish and become the independent, self-respecting person you are meant to be.

How This Book Will Benefit You

In this book, you will learn the importance of setting safe, fail-proof boundaries that will ensure you find success and happiness. These boundaries will not only be those that help to protect you on a physical level, such as your resources, property, and your body, but they are invaluable for defining your emotions, thoughts, values, and your beliefs.

There are plenty of useful tips on how to recognize the potential dangers of someone transgressing your boundaries as well as advice on how best to circumvent these unpleasant issues. You will discover valuable clues on how to establish personal boundaries to protect your own wellbeing, with advice on how best to handle infringements of your boundaries by friends, family members, as well as coworkers, including your boss.

This book will empower you to set realistic boundaries for yourself, your family members, friends, and co-workers without running the gambit of offending anyone. You will learn how and when to stand up for yourself so that you can command respect from those around you without falling prey to any unnecessary guilt or judgement.

A Bit About the Author

Having worked with many others who have struggled to put boundaries in place for over 20 years in my field, I wish to share my extensive knowledge and understanding of the importance and value of setting boundaries in your relationships. My vast experience and success with helping others overcome their struggles with their self-worth as a result of poor communication and lack of boundary setting have ensured that I have a vested interest in your happiness and well-being.

My love of my fellow humans, and my desire to give you valuable tips and share important advice to help you understand the positive aspects of learning to structure realistic boundaries in your life, is what drives me to share my expertise with you.

Without further ado, let's discover the importance of boundary setting to realize your potential happiness and health, so that you can start living out the best version of you!

Chapter 1: All About Boundaries

When we think of boundaries, we tend to think of a figurative line that we draw with others. A line that clearly says to others what we can tolerate and what we won't tolerate in a relationship. Perhaps you've been confused with when to draw this line, or perhaps you may have never thought you needed a line to begin with.

As we grow and mature, we may start to become more aware of the necessity of setting boundaries for successful relationships when we start seeing the pitfalls of not having any established. You may at first be worried that boundary setting will have a negative impact on your relationships with others or think that it may change the relationship completely.

However, more often than not, setting boundaries with others will allow others to truly appreciate you and the relationship, instead of taking your existence or good nature for granted.

To better understand boundaries, consider them instead as the rules that you've set in the game of life. These rules help you navigate the course to your own happiness and success, whilst also allowing others who enter the game to know where to start and how to continue. Without these rules, the game can certainly be played, however what you'll find is that others will start defining the course to your happiness and steer you off track. This may not be intentional, but without any rules or controls in place, it is very easy for all the players to forget that the game belongs to *you*.

Boundary setting isn't about exercising power or setting yourself center stage. Far from it. Instead, what you'll find is that having boundaries is as much about giving what you are prepared to give, as it is about taking what others are happy to provide you. The balance in this, though often tricky, is what will ultimately define the relationship that you have with others.

Why We Need Boundaries

When we have boundaries, we ensure that all our efforts, time, and goodwill are protected and respected by those around us. In turn, we will see our relationships become more robust and endure over time.

Boundaries serve as protection against others who will continuously take advantage of you without any consideration to your thoughts, feelings, emotions or wellbeing. Being without boundaries makes you easy prey for losing your rights and freedom to others who will demand and take more of your time, patience, energy, and support than they deserve.

For example, you may have decided to help out a friend by letting them stay at your apartment free of rent until they find a job. However, once they do find a job you notice that they make no efforts to move out despite having previously agreed to it. Perhaps they're in a financial situation that you're not aware of? Or, maybe they're looking but no place is suitable? Then you start noticing the frequent night outs and weekend getaways, as well as the constant shopping that must be costing a fortune. Should you just accept the live-in and start asking for their fair share of rent? You become stressed as you simply don't know how best to tackle this.

When you have a clear idea of what is permissible in your life, you are better prepared to standing up for yourself by standing firm on your principles and values. Boundaries give you the confidence to live your life as you choose and not be subjected to any abuse, whether physical, verbal, emotional or psychological.

At times the people who are closest to you may be just as guilty to making you feel unsafe or uncomfortable in their company, or they may make you feel insecure in yourself and the relationship that you have with them. Such transgressions can slowly change your sense of self-worth. It can make you lose trust in others as well as yourself, inhibiting you from meeting new people, establishing new connections, or even the ability to interact with others on a basic level.

When you have clear boundaries in place, it's hard for others not to respect you. This is because having boundaries indicates that you know what you want in life, how you want to be treated, as well as what you are worth. Knowing your true worth means that you won't accept or tolerate when others take you for granted. This allows you to recognize those who genuinely appreciates you and your relationship with them, so that you can begin investing your valuable time and effort on those who truly matter.

Healthy relationships can only exist when there are boundaries in place. When you become aware of this, it is very hard for you to not start thinking about what your boundaries are with others. The relationships that are grounded on firm, clear and respectful boundaries are those that will grow and mature with you. This means that boundaries are not static but are flexible as they change with time and circumstances.

A World with No Boundaries

Let's imagine a world where there are no boundaries in place. Would it be as chaotic as if there were no traffic lights in place to guide those who are driving about? Would it be absolute mayhem and pandemonium, with accidents galore? You'd be surprised to find that the answer is not as dramatic or as exciting.

Just as boundaries are not designed for one to exercise power over others, the lack of boundaries causes changes of a more subtle and subversive nature.

When there is a lack of boundary setting, the need to address matters no matter how significant or insignificant becomes almost inconsequential. This unfortunately lends itself to needless emotional, psychological and sometimes physical suffering. By the time one realizes that boundaries are needed, it may already be too late, as the pain and suffering have already been inflicted to all those involved.

Amy and Greg

Amy and Greg had been dating for just over two weeks. Amy has never been the affectionate kind, but Greg would at every opportunity try to display public affection when they are together. Amy had never been in a relationship before, but at 24, her friends were either married or in a serious relationship, and she didn't want to be teased as the single friend forever.

On a Friday night, after a romantic dinner, Greg invited himself up to her apartment. Amy had sex for the first time, but she did not enjoy it. She chalked this experience up to it being her first time, so she decided not to answer honestly when Greg asked her how she felt afterwards. As the relationship continued, sex became frequent, much more than Amy was prepared for, and Amy found that she would dread it so much, that each time it happened she would be anxious and counting down to when the act would finally finish. Amy wasn't sure how to ever bring up this topic with Greg for fear of hurting his feelings. However, not having the honest conversation about how frequently they should have sex, and how Greg could satisfy her so that she could enjoy it, meant that sex became something that was both scary and painful.

Amy and Greg's relationship lasted well into the following year, and Amy would find herself accepting Greg's proposal for marriage. However, at the back of her mind, Amy would always wonder what she was really missing out on every time her friends would discuss their own intimate experiences with her.

Jane and Margaret

Jane had just come home from the hospital after giving birth to her very first child. She was absolutely ready to seek rest in her own bed and relax within the confines of her safe haven.

When Jane got out of the car, she was shocked to see the sight of her in-laws standing by the open doorway. Jane realized that before her pregnancy she had never established boundaries and simply tolerated random visits in order to keep the peace. Now, however, these unannounced "drop-ins" no longer feel appropriate, but she had no idea how to tell her in-laws to leave.

As she welcomed the in-laws into her home, the first thing her mother-in-law Margaret commented on was how she was holding her newborn incorrectly. Jane had to bite her tongue as Margaret took her newborn son from her and proceeded to coo the baby away from her and towards her husband, who was standing awkwardly by the kitchen.

Jane tried to give her husband a look to signal that she was tired and needed to go bed, and hopefully have his parents leave immediately. However, the look was not returned, and Jane found that she would be entertaining the in-laws for upwards of an hour, before they would go home.

Unfortunately, this would continue every few days. These few days turned into weeks, and then months. Soon Jane found that she needed to organize the spare room downstairs for Margaret to permanently move into, at which point she could no longer differentiate whether the resentment she felt stemmed from her mother-in-law or if it had been from her husband who never took her side.

Joyce and Pamela

Joyce and Pamela have been colleagues for over six months working at the local supermarket. Joyce, whilst not exactly the meek and shy type, is still rather reserved and prefers not to share her personal life with others. Pamela, on the other hand, can be guilty of oversharing, and enjoys prying into everybody's business.

Recently, Joyce's father had passed away, and so she was quieter than usual during her shifts at work. Pamela, sensing the change, went on to repeatedly ask Joyce what the matter was and if she was okay. Unable to find the words to tell Pamela to stop, and also still feeling the emotions of her father's passing, Joyce ends up breaking down just as their manager walks by. Seeing the emotional Joyce, the manager immediately tells Pamela to leave Joyce alone and mind her own business. Pamela tries to defend herself, but the manager will have nothing of it.

After this incident, Pamela is a noticeably different person and doesn't approach Joyce or anyone else for that matter, unless required for work purposes. Whilst Joyce enjoys the newfound quiet in the store, she cannot help but feel partly responsible for Pamela's now withdrawn personality. Joyce doesn't know if she should be apologizing to Pamela for not letting her know she needed space when she was going through a period of grieving. However, now she feels that it is too late, with Pamela avoiding her at all costs.

When we look at the examples above, I'm sure you'll agree that we cannot pin the blame on any one individual. Every party had the chance to make changes in the relationship, but the lack of boundary setting meant that none of them knew where to start. In the case of Amy and Greg, Amy's continued deference to her husband to have the conversation with his parents, meant that she missed the opportunity to let her honest feelings be known. The resentment that she was left with ends up being shared with him, despite the issue originally being with her in-laws.

No doubt, there can also be consequences that impact others and not just the person whose boundaries have been infringed upon. In the example with Joyce and Pamela, what we see is that by Joyce not setting her boundaries in place, she inadvertently changes the bright and talkative Pamela into a quiet and withdrawn individual. Pamela goes on to learn the hard way what it can mean to transgress onto someone's personal space without their tacit approval – a lesson that she won't be forgetting any time soon.

We can only imagine if the necessary boundaries had been set at the start of each of the relationships, or from when it was first discovered that there was a need for one, how much differently things could have played out for all those involved.

What Does Successful Boundaries Look Like?

Success can only be achieved when we know what success looks like. Successful boundary setting can have impact big or small, but the constant in all this is that you will feel immensely proud of yourself once you see others respecting you for having them. Boundaries don't need to be complicated, but they do need to be clear so that others know exactly where they stand with you.

Marissa and the Director

Marissa is known to be easy-going and kind in her workplace. She is a junior developer in one of the larger companies in her area, with the goal of becoming a leading developer in the next 12 months.

During one of the meetings where a number of colleagues were running late, she overhears the Director mentioning that he was craving for a coffee. Feeling the effects of a 4 o'clock meeting, she decided she needed one also and offered to get the Director one as a kind gesture. Marissa received thanks, and the afternoon meeting soon started and continued on without a hitch.

In the follow-up meeting which occurred a few days later, Marissa was again asked by the same Director to go on a coffee run. It was 12 o'clock, and Marissa doesn't drink coffee before lunch, so she found it odd that out of everyone in the room she had been asked to make this particular errand. She then remembered what had happened in the last meeting and realized that she may have caused the director to misunderstand what her role at the company was.

Marissa knew that she needed to rectify this as soon as she can, lest she be turned into the coffee girl, or worse be judged as a brown-noser. She went ahead and bought the coffee, however, once the meeting finished, she asked if she could have a moment with the Director alone.

She addressed the misunderstanding about the coffee and made it clear that whilst she was very happy to buy the two coffees for him, should he wish for another, it may be best to ask his PA instead.

This would be the last time Marissa would be asked to go for a coffee run. But to her surprise, her relationship with the Director only improved from this experience, as he would later tell her that he found her honesty and straightforwardness a refreshing change in the office.

Here we have a great example of setting boundaries early and not allowing misunderstandings to take place. The added surprise of a new friendship between Marissa and the Director also showcases how fortuitous occurrences can appear as a result of good boundary setting. While it may be a scary thought to set boundaries with those with whom you are not familiar with, or even those with whom you can love dearly, having the courage to set boundaries can yield positive outcomes that you may have never anticipated before.

Setting boundaries is also beneficial for your own wellbeing. These are the limits that you set in place so that you do not go on to hurt or neglect yourself when things get busy or hectic in life. Being able to draw a line with yourself on what you will tolerate means that you are willing to put yourself first by prioritizing your needs, your health and your own happiness.

John

John is a truck driver who is used to working long days and nights, alone on the road and with no one beside him. He has a wife and two children back home but being on the road so much meant that he was rarely home to see them.

From a young age, John was taught that being a man meant being the provider for the family.

That the more money you made now meant the less you'd need to work when you got older.

It was his younger son's fifth birthday on October 1st, and he'd missed it yet again. That year he also missed his son's first day at school as well as his older 13-year-old's first marathon win. John only needed to hear from his wife that his son had been waiting for him to come home that day to say, "happy birthday", for which he had missed, to be assaulted by an enormous pang of guilt and regret. He'd been working for over 20 years of his life and he felt that he had achieved nothing and was only missing out on both his children's precious childhood.

That week, John requested for a six-month break from work. He had enough long service leave to cover for this period, and his boss was only too eager to have his most hardworking staff finally take some leave, that the request was approved instantly.

John's kids were ecstatic the first few days that they saw him home, but soon became suspicious as their dad had never taken any leave from work, ever. He enjoyed convincing his kids that, no, he didn't "get fired from his job", and that no, he wasn't "taken over by aliens," that he didn't even notice how quickly time was going by.

The six months flew by and John found himself back at work and having never-ending conversations with his boss and colleagues about all the things that he did with his family.

"I'm so glad you took that leave," said his boss, halfway through him recounting what had happened to his older son during their first camping trip.

John looked at his boss in surprise.

"You sound like a completely changed person," his boss continued. "You sound happy."

How to Recognize the Need for

Boundaries

Now that you can see what life can be like with and without boundaries, you may be still suspecting whether you really need to set boundaries in your life. Take a moment to ask yourself the below and be honest with your answers.

1. Is there anyone with whom you feel doesn't respect or appreciate you or the things that you do?
2. Do you think the above is due to a lack of communication or honesty between you?
3. Do you want to improve or strengthen the relationship because you value the individual and what they bring to the table?

If a person came to mind when you were answering these questions, chances are you have been feeling that something has been amiss in the relationship, but you just never expected that to be boundaries. You may be convinced now more than ever that you are lacking boundaries in your life. If you're ever confused, try to remember to ask yourself those three questions when dealing with those around you. That way you'll be able to identify when boundaries are missing and make efforts to set them before it's too late.

Now, here's the decider for whether you have the ability in you to set boundaries successfully:

4. Are you prepared to be firm in the boundaries that you choose to set?
5. Are you prepared to walk away should your boundaries not be respected?

Being firm in your resolve is absolutely paramount to ensuring that your boundaries are effective and likewise respected. Though it may be difficult in the face of some with whom you may have had a long history with, such as a parent, a childhood friend, or a lifelong partner, holding your ground and standing tall when your boundaries have been infringed upon tells them that you not only have respect for yourself, but also of the relationship to be able to voice your opinions so honestly and so openly.

That being said, there can be concessions made so that both parties can reach a peaceful agreement. However, being flexible is not the same as someone who says "yes" all the time, so make sure that the compromises that you do make are fundamentally acceptable to you. Should this not be the case, then by all means have the courage to walk out of this relationship, as it no longer holds any regard to your needs and wants. This will only result in a toxic dynamic, something that you will be glad to be leaving behind.

Chapter 2: Getting Started with Setting Boundaries

While talking to my clients I often ask them what they really want out of life or their relationships. Most of them are happy to complain and bring me up to speed on all the things about their relationship or circumstances that irritate, annoy, or frustrate them. Sadly, very few can give a clear indication of their expectations. The starting point usually begins with questions about their values. So, how do you define your values?

Everything you believe is important and worthwhile in your life, including the way you live, treat your family and friends, how you view your job and the amount of effort you give to every aspect of your life encompasses your values. The way in which you behave and the things you do should match your values if you want to be happy and successful. It's when there's a discrepancy between what you believe and how you act that trouble begins to brew.

Identify and Understand Your Core Values

To begin, it's important that we get into the habit of applying conscious effort to identifying our values, so that we can have a better chance of making good plans and sensible decisions. It is good practice to also consider changing your lifestyle to honor your values so that you are more likely to find enjoyment in everything that you do.

Understanding your values will help you set up worthwhile boundaries that will act as protection against unwanted drama later in your life. For example, if you value your family life, then you will resent working long hours and not being able to spend as much time with the family as you may wish to. On the other hand, if you are goal-oriented at work, taking time off to watch your kid play baseball may be an irritation you can do without. Values drive the way in which we live, so it is important that you have a firm grasp of the types of values that you hold.

Remember, values are not static but can change with us as we mature. When you start your working career, you may place a high value on money, wealth, and success. Later, when you have children, your values may shift to encompass your family. When this occurs, you may find yourself placing greater value on spending quality time with your loved ones or working harder to provide for them.

Defining your values can therefore be quite a challenging task.

To help you identify your values, you need to first be honest with your experiences and your emotions. Have a go at answering the questions below, as your answers will help you in identifying what your values are.

1. *Think about a time when someone made you happy. What did they do to make you happy?*
2. *Think about a time when someone upset you. What was it that they did to upset you?*
3. *Think about a time when you were most proud. What made you feel proud?*
4. *Think about a time when you felt most fulfilled. What fulfilled you?*

From your answers, you should now be more aware of what your values are. Grab a pen, if you've not already done so, and start jotting down the values that correlate to each of your answers.

For example, if in the first question you answered that you were most happy when your family was able to spend time together overseas, then one of your values would be family and loyalty, etc.

You might end up with a table such as the below, or maybe a list that is a lot longer. When you've finished jotting down all your values, circle the values that resonates the most with you – these will be your core values.

My Values

Family	Honesty	*Loyalty*	*Commitment*
Positivity	Passion	*Fairness*	Accountability
Open-Mindedness	Authenticity	Equality	Autonomy

duty, service, respect

Remember, the values that you choose should give you a deep sense of integrity and worthiness. You should feel secure about your

respect for others peoples property.
- working on - tollerance, respect for others
- open mindedness.
- compromise

choices and know that to exercise your values in every area of your life, you will find balance, success, and happiness.

Deciding the Right Boundaries for You

Now that you have your values figured out, you are in a great position to begin deciding on the boundaries you wish to have in your relationships.

Based on your values, you should have a clearer idea of your wants and expectations from others. Our unique characteristics lead us to identify with different values. What we want and desire will, therefore, differ with others, which is why you will seldom find someone with identical values and wants such as yours! That being said, you will need to learn how to compromise with others whose wants and values are different from your own.

But here's the thing: just like how you won't force your wants and values on others, you don't have to feel obligated to accept other people's wants and values where these clash with your own.

Boundaries Should Align to your Core Values

Boundaries only make sense when they are congruent with what you value and hold dear. For example, if one of your core values is loyalty, then it only makes sense that the boundary that you set with others begin and end with your definition of what loyalty means.

If loyalty to you means that your partner cannot be with another person of the opposite sex no matter the situation, then the line that you draw with them could be that they cannot be alone with a person of the opposite sex unless you are present. However, if your definition of loyalty is simply that they make it known to everyone around them that they are in a relationship with you, you might not mind them going to the movies with the person of the opposite sex, so long as they tell you about it beforehand.

There is no right or wrong definition to what your core values mean as each of us are unique in our own special way and have our own interpretation and understanding of the values that we hold dear. When we understand our values and align them to our boundaries, it becomes easier to detect when there is a breach or violation of these boundaries because our internal compass will resound loudly.

That being said, make sure to go easy on yourself because boundaries can change over time as we grow and develop into ourselves. You may find that when you were younger you valued fun and humor, and so you could tolerate your friends teasing of strangers so long as you had a good laugh. Once you are older, however, you may come to realize that respect for everyone's differences has become more important to you, and so you may find yourself distancing from the group who have continued to make fun of others without regard.

So long as you know what is important to you, the boundaries that you have should be safeguarding these precious values that you hold. Other people's judgements and opinions may make you doubt the boundaries that you've set out, but by being honest with yourself, you can trust that you are making the most suitable and relevant boundaries that will work best for you.

Know your Limits

Everyone has a threshold when it comes to the absolute amount of unwanted and undeserved criticism, anger, pain or suffering that they will allow others to inflict upon them. When this threshold is reached, it triggers your internal defense mechanism, much like the fight and flight response, that compels you to take action for self-preservation. If you struggle to know what boundaries you should have in your life, look no further than at your own personal limits, as they can dictate what you will and won't accept when dealing with others.

Being able to stand up for yourself under challenging circumstances is an integral part of showcasing what your limits are with others. All too often, many of us choose the non-confrontational route. In the long run, this is more likely to be the least effective response. The main reason for this reaction is the sense of guilt you may experience when you say "no" to things you don't want to do, because you believe that your negative response may cause the other person discomfort, unhappiness or a feeling of being neglected. Understanding your limits allow you to overcome that guilt as the alternative is to hurt yourself, which as we know is never healthy. Knowing your limits also empowers you to rise above the resistance you may experience towards yourself and can encourage you to seek support from others who may be in a similar situation to you.

Enacting your limits can be as easy, or as hard, as the two-letter word, "no". When you allow yourself the power to say "no" to others, you are being honest and true to yourself. Saying "no" takes courage, and willingness to bravely stand your ground. Once you have mastered its use, "no" can open opportunities or close the door to potential dangers.

Most people understand the meaning of "no" and on the whole, they will respect you for your honesty. By knowing your own limits of what you will accept or not accept, you are putting yourself first for a change. When you learn to say "no", you automatically consider the importance of the situation with a direct reference to you. This is a great start on your journey to self-care and appreciation!

Saying "no" allows you to safeguard what you hold dear, protects you from harm that others may knowingly or unknowingly inflict upon you, and it prevents the very easy opportunity for others to take you or your kindness for granted. Keep in mind, though, that not everyone will accept "no" graciously. When this occurs, make sure you're honest with yourself to understand and determine what you want and what you're willing to compromise on, before you decide to make any concessions.

Just as "no" can pack a punch for such a small two letter-word, the word "yes" can just be as significant when deciding what you will allow and won't allow from others. Knowing what you want and giving yourself the option to take on opportunities can all arise from saying "yes" when the chance presents itself.

Once again, there is no right or wrong way to approach this. What you need to do is have an honest conversation with yourself and allow your inner thoughts and feelings take over. Let yourself be guided by this and don't allow anyone to put their voices in your head, so as to project their needs and wants onto you.

Lisa and Mary

It was nearing the end of October, so the planning for the annual office Christmas Party was quickly coming up. Lisa was always the organizer of this event as Christmas excited her greatly.

One afternoon, Mary, her colleague, after piling another set of invoices on Lisa's desk decided to hang around to see if she could get a sneak peek of this year's events.

"So, what theme will we be going with this year, Lisa?" Mary asked, unconsciously moving some of the contents on Lisa's desk as she leaned against it.

Lisa wasn't sure what was going on this year, but the invoices just didn't seem to stop! She had about four piles to enter into the system, and this new batch that Mary had just given her was making her feel all sorts of stress! Not to mention, her sister had asked her a favor to babysit her nephew for two weeks, so that she could go on her first overseas trip with her husband in God knows how long! That's right, she needed to clock off soon to go to the grocers so that she could be home in time to make dinner for a picky, annoying, 8-year-old brat!

"Oh, Mary," Lisa groused, "I have not even had a chance to think about the Christmas party! Everything's just so hectic right now!"

"But, Lisa," said Mary, oblivious to her colleague's plight, "if you don't get started now, we're going to lose out on the really good places and restaurants. Everyone's making reservations now in time for December!"

Lisa could feel the disappointment in Mary's tone, and she felt frustrated that she wasn't able to find any time to organize the one event that she loved. But right now just wasn't the time! She knew that she would be running around looking like a headless chicken if she had to take on the responsibility of planning the office Christmas party alongside what was already on her plate.

"I know, Mary," said Lisa. "But I just can't at the moment. There's a lot going on right now, and I just don't think I can handle having to plan it right now."

Mary finally took stock of Lisa's desk and saw the mess that was there. Piles and piles of invoices, with post-its and pens strewn about. "Wow," said Mary, "you *do* have a lot going on." Then, after a pause asked, "well, would you mind if I organized this year's Christmas party, instead?"

Lisa felt a wave of relief rush over her. She didn't realize how much not being able to organize the party was weighing her down!

Now, she felt much better knowing that the celebration would still continue.

"That would be amazing!" Lisa said.

"No dramas! I've got plenty of time on my hand – this will be fun!"

"If you need any ideas or suggestions, let me know, okay? Once I get on top of all this, I'd be more than happy to help!"

"Don't sweat it," said Mary. "Focus on what you need to do and leave this party with me!"

Recognize Your Emotional Needs and Those of Others

When deciding on your boundaries, you need to consider the emotional needs of you and those around you. Our emotional needs are often the most powerful of our needs that drive us to perform, act, behave, and react in certain ways to specific situations. Being able to recognize what we need so that we can achieve happiness, fulfilment and peace in our lives, is what will center us and allow us to respond to others in positive ways, and vice versa. This will allow us to maintain our boundaries while respecting those of the other person.

Ask yourself what your emotional needs are, as they will be different for everyone. Below are a few to get you started:

Acceptance

Feeling accepted by those around you can play a huge part in how you see yourself, and how successful you may feel. No one can realistically expect themselves to be accepted by everyone around them. However, amongst those who do matter, the feeling of not being accepted can cause emotions ranging from sadness, feelings of inferiority, frustration and alienation.

When someone values acceptance above all else, they may offer their support and services in abundance. However, be careful what their intentions may be, as unhealthy cravings for acceptance can lead to expectations of one's attention being reciprocated. If this is not something you share, be sure to set your boundaries early and clearly.

Validation

Validation often comes from others providing the seal of approval to you, your actions, your thoughts, and ultimately your worth. It can also come from within, when you feel content with your success and the choices that you have made in life. Being validated can boost your confidence, allowing you to feel 'right' and 'worthwhile' at the same time. When you don't feel validated, you may feel lost, confused, of little worth or even a failure.

For those who crave validation, it may be constant encouragements or reassurances that they seek from those around them. Being sure to pay real compliments should the need arises, will go a long way.

Autonomy

Some people will love their independence and enjoy the control they have over their own decisions and their own life. Having autonomy affords one the confidence to feel their own worth, and in turn allows them to respect other's boundaries for seeking help and assistance.

Autonomy can be felt over one's career, finances, body, thoughts and feelings. Keep in mind though that just because someone has autonomy over one facet of their life, you cannot assume that they have autonomy over all other facets that make up who they are. For example, you can be financially independent, but also career dependent at the same time.

Security

Feelings of security can manifest in relationships such as family, friends and one's intimate partner. It can also be found in one's career, finances and reputation. Cravings for security is often associated with the need to seek comfort and ease in people and/or things, in order to feel safe and assured.

Insecurity is when you face a constant threat that what you have will be taken away from you. This can be your time, your money, your career, your lover, etc. For those who are faced with insecurity, the issue is often a lack of confidence in themselves and those around them.

Trust

In all good relationships, you will often find trust between all parties. This includes relationships with others as well as yourself. Trusting yourself and trusting what you bring to the table can find yourself exuding confidence that will draw others towards you.

Trust and security often go hand in hand. If you have trust in others, you will feel secure with what you have. On the contrary, a lack of trust often breeds insecurity, which will lead to various other issues that causes stress, pain and needless anxiety.

Empathy

The ability to put yourself into someone else's shoes in order to understand how they feel, is an essential part of any worthwhile relationship, whether this is of a personal or romantic nature. By taking the time to identify with someone's feelings, you are better able to accept their unique challenges and can offer your support when it is needed.

Priority

You should be your own number one priority. Your thoughts, feelings and emotions should be the first thing you consider with everything that you do. That being said, if this is true for everyone, others will also believe that they hold the same importance in your life.

Being able to understand that others will want to be treated as if they are the most important person in the world can be a huge challenge for us all. However, by showing empathy, interest, and genuine concern in your relationships, you will succeed in making others feel special, unique, and cared for.

Connection

When you make an effort to reach out to others, you allow yourself to connect with these people in order to form personal, social, and emotional bonds with them. Being able to relate to others shows that you have well-defined boundaries that give you the courage to interact without fear of prejudice.

Connection goes a long way. It gives us the sense of belonging in this vast world of ours. It is also what will anchor us in our relationships and is one of the special things that can develop and strengthen its hold with time.

Space

Though connecting with others is important for one's emotional well-being, so too is the need for personal space and distance. Relationships thrive when time is set aside for personal privacy and peace. It allows you to take stock of your current situation, reconnect with your inner self, and learn to appreciate the other more the next time you see them.

When you don't give yourself or others space, you will quickly find yourself feeling overwhelmed without knowing the reason why. By recognizing when you need to take a break from others, you afford yourself with the ability to think with better clarity, resulting in far greater decision-making upon your return.

Managing Potential Infringements to Your Boundaries

Protecting your boundaries from infringements is critical to maintaining the health of your relationships. When you find that one of your boundaries has been infringed upon for the first time, you may feel unsure of whether to address the violation or to simply let it slide. This may be because the violation is small or seemingly innocent, or maybe it's because the person is a first-time offender.

If you are torn between saying something or simply ignoring it, you need to ask yourself the following:

> 1. *To what extent did the action infringe upon your core values?*

This is the most important question you need to answer every time an infringement occurs. Remember, boundaries are based on your core values. When an infringement is small or negligible, chances are your values were only neglected for a short moment in time. However, if the incident demonstrates a complete disregard for what your core values are, then you simply cannot avoid having this confrontation.

This doesn't mean expressing anger or starting an argument. Rather, be calm and reasonable, and express how the violation of the boundary has made you feel. Perhaps the person wasn't aware that they had crossed the line with you, or perhaps they had no idea how important this value means to you. Having an honest and open conversation will help reinforce the boundary that you had established with the person, as well as ensure that the infringement won't be happening again. If it does happen again, it will be a reflection of the person's inability to respect your boundaries and you may want to reevaluate the relationship that you both share.

If you don't believe that your core values have been infringed upon, you may need a few more questions to determine whether this is an issue that is worth raising. Two simple questions that you will want to ask yourself is the following:

1. *Under what circumstance did this infringement occur?*
2. *How often has this infringement occurred?*

Try to recall the incident and determine if the perpetrator was in the right mental or emotional state when the infringement occurred. That is, were they drunk, stressed or upset? Under the most trying conditions even the best of us can be found capable of demonstrating ugly actions and behaviors that we wouldn't ordinarily display on a normal day.

If the person was indeed in an altered mental or emotional state, does the infringement occur often? We may be tempted to excuse poor behavior when someone is not themselves, however, if they are often found to be not themselves, or if they show signs of emotional imbalance, then you can be sure that these infringements will continue and can likely escalate to put you in an even more uncomfortable situation in the future.

Your answers should make you feel comfortable that your boundaries are respected. If you have suspicions that they are not, then communication is definitely required so as to avoid misunderstandings taking place.

Chapter 3: Boundaries for Friends

Setting boundaries with your friends is essential to the development and survival of true, lasting friendships that will afford growth and happiness to all those involved. Often, we tend to assume that boundaries are not required or expected in a good friendship regardless of whether the friendship is platonic or intimate. This is because we may have expectations that our needs and wants are automatically understood by those closest to us and feel that boundaries in this relationship are unnecessary and can provide no additional value. However, acting on this assumption only denies those closest to us the opportunity to gain a deeper understanding of our true inner self, as well as preventing the relationship to grow and mature with us.

All Friendships Require Boundaries

It's important to know that for every friendship to remain healthy, viable, and respectful, both parties need to set firm, clear boundaries. All too often, boundaries are viewed with negative cynicism especially by those friends who feel insecure or who may display abnormally possessive qualities. By creating sensible boundaries in a friendship, you inevitably encourage the development of positive self-esteem and the growth of confidence in the alliance.

Being confident to ensure your friends understand who you are and what you want from them is fundamental for the growth and survival of your friendship. It's also important to make sure your friends understand your beliefs, limits, and values, and that you reciprocate this accordingly.

Any friendship without boundaries is doomed to fail from the get-go, just as general success and happiness in life cannot be achieved without clear-cut rules and guidelines. Boundaries can be small and insignificant, but without them, you encourage other people to take advantage either knowingly or otherwise of your goodwill, kind heart and your generosity.

Healthy Friendships Require Clear Boundaries

You may think that your best friend should automatically know your feelings, wants, expectations, and understand you through and through. Sadly, this is never often the case. No two people are the same in any way. You each react differently to specific stimuli and though you may enjoy a wide variety of similar activities, foods, music, and sports, you remain two separate individuals with innate fears and likes specific to your personality.

You may feel setting boundaries will ruin the friendship because it suggests that you don't trust that your friend knows who you are, never mind how long the relationship has been going for. However, what you are doing is not dissimilar to an NBA player closing their eyes when at the free throw line and shooting, hoping that luck and experience gets them the hoop. By offering no guidelines for what your needs and wants are to your friends, you're essentially allowing them to guesswork their way through and then permitting them excuses for when transgressions occur.

When boundaries are clearly defined and respected, the need for physical walls and barricades falls away. You are able to be honest with each other, and trust each other more, because abiding by these boundaries have proven that you both know what it takes to keep the relationship going.

Crossing the boundary by invitation or mutual consent is a wonderful way of demonstrating faith and true respect for each other. However, deliberate violation of the boundary creates only anger, fear, and confusion and in the end may result in violent counteraction. By always asking for permission first, you allow your friends to feel safe and comfortable around you, and vice versa, which will only continue to strengthen the relationship and the mutual respect that you have for each other.

Communicate Clearly

Boundaries should be fair and just, without using emotional, physical, or mental blackmail to cajole your friends into adhering to them. For example, "I'll kill myself if you go shopping without me!" Using such strong language to try and manipulate your friends into behaving according to your standards isn't going to keep your relationship on a good, healthy footing. Though boundaries are important, forceful language like, "you must," or "you will have to", even if it is in a joking manner, is never effective and can even put unnecessary strain in the relationship. Instead, rephrase your request so that it reads polite without being condescending, firm without being bossy, and straightforward to avoid misunderstanding.

When asking your friend for help, try to avoid vague instructions like, "help me fix my car when you can!" Be specific so that the correct message is sent and correctly received. Try rephrasing the message as, "can you help me fix my car by this week? If not, I'm happy to just go to the car shop, instead." This will let your friend know that there is a clear deadline, but that you are happy to seek alternate help if they are busy. Your friend also won't feel pressured to help if they are truly busy themselves. Believing your friend will automatically know your boundaries just because the two of you are close and may have been friends for a long time will cause unnecessary misunderstanding, so try to avoid this at all costs.

Allow Space Between You

Setting boundaries can include allowing yourself space and time to pursue your own interests as well as ensuring you make it known when you feel disrespected or that your boundaries have been infringed upon. Likewise, this is a two-way street so your friends should be allowed the same opportunity to discuss what makes them uncomfortable, uneasy, or just plain irritated.

If you feel you need a break from a consistent amount of phone calls and catchups with your friends, let them know you need some time for yourself. But also make it known when you will be ready for the next time you will be able to see them, so that they won't take it personally and can give you the space that you need.

Respect Each Other's Belongings

A common theme that have incurred friendship breakdowns often stem from when one party takes possessions of things or items that belong to the other without permission. Items may be tangible, such as money or perhaps a new pair of shoes; or intangible such as time or certain already established bonds.

If you find your friend taking and using things that are rightfully yours without first asking your permission, you need to set up boundaries right away to protect your belongings. Similarly, you need to make sure that you don't cross those lines you've set yourself so that you can demonstrate how important those boundaries are to you.

Scenario 1

Your friend has made it clear that you may not use anything that belongs to them without their permission. You have also agreed to put this boundary in place. Now, you find that while they are away, your car won't start so you immediately borrow your friend's car to run your errands.

No matter how small and insignificant you believe the boundary to be, it is of paramount importance that you adhere to the rules of the relationship. Firstly, by agreeing to this boundary you have promised to abide by it. Your disrespect for your friend's boundary can make them lose trust in you and your friendship. Once the first layer of trust is broken, it becomes easier to breach other seemingly smaller promises that you have made with each other, and soon it becomes unclear for both where exactly the boundaries are.

When you are in a situation where you know you may be going against the rules of the friendship, always let the other person know so that even if it's a one-time rule break, you receive the permission from them directly.

Scenario 2

Your office colleagues have planned an end-of-month function to celebrate someone's birthday. You purchase a gift for the occasion. Your friend gets jealous because they feel your choice of gift is better than what they received from you for their birthday some months ago. To avoid drama, you go out and change the gift for something else.

You have unknowingly succumbed to your friend's jealousy and have ended up being emotionally blackmailed into changing your mind. Your friend may not be aware that their response to this gift has made you feel uncomfortable and have forced you to change the gift as a result. If this is unaddressed, a lingering resentment may occur that will eventually pop its head during the next big argument.

Let your friend know in the first instance that the gift bears no weighting on how you view the relationship. But, now that you know that your friend also prefers this gift, you will make sure that for their next birthday you will make a similar purchase or one that they will definitely like better.

Identifying Different Types of Abuse

Are you that friend who is always called upon to help out when the going gets tough? Or are you more the type who only gets invited to outings when another has bailed last minute?

When we're with the people that we like, we like to be generous with our time, patience, care and goodwill, without any expectations that these things are returned in equal amounts. Being friends with others means that there is always that relationship of give and take, so you don't measure who does more for the other as long as when the time arrives for when you need the love and support, you know that they are there for you.

When you start to find yourself questioning the authenticity of the friendship, it may be that you are starting to feel that it is always *you* who is doing the giving.

Are they friends with me because they like me? Or are they friends with me because they need something from me?

This can occur when you feel that you are simply not being appreciated and the time, patience, care and goodwill that you selflessly provide to your friends are being abused.

Abuse from those closest to you can take on many forms. It isn't always violence in action, or words laced with contempt. Abuse can be slight, and it can be subtle. You may not recognize it at face value, but you might feel it strongly inside of you that something just isn't quite right.

Take a look at the following scenarios and see if any of these resonate with you. If you connect with one (or many) of them, note the response so that you can start protecting yourself from the needless abuse of others.

The People Pleaser

Your friends constantly make demands of your time and support and you find that you will provide these without question. When you're unable to hang out or spend time with your them, rather than trying to be understanding you are instead accused of not caring or valuing the friendship. You discover that your needs and wants are expected to take a backseat, as your friend's welfare should always come first.

Response

You've become subjected to the needs and wants of your friends without any considerations of your own, thereby allowing yourself to be taken advantage of. When you are made to feel guilty of caring about your own welfare then this signals that there is an expectation mismatch between those involved.

Have a good, honest conversation with your friend and let them know that you are very happy to be there for them and provide the support that they need, but that there are limits to what you can do for them. Explain to them what your expectations are of the relationship and let them know how you feel when your needs and wants are being ignored.

The Problem Fixer

You're the friend who's the "fixer" of all situations, and the go-to alibi when one is needed. Every time your mates are in a tricky situation, you know that you'll be called to bail them out. You've been the shield that they've used when they're in a quarrel with their partner or the excuse thrown in situations when they want to avoid attending events or functions. Irrespective of the type of scenario, you are the one they turn to in times of need.

Response

If you begin to feel uncomfortable being the person to always solve your friends' issues, you need to speak up and let them know about this discomfort. You may feel good knowing that you are needed and relied upon but be careful when this type of dependence hinders the opportunity for any type of growth.

Ask yourself how often these situations occur, and if your friend has learnt anything from the predicaments that they are trying to avoid. When you always help solve your friend's problems, you run the risk of removing their ability to start thinking for themselves.

The Peacemaker

Every time there is an argument, you are called to become the mediator in the situation. However, when you try your best to offer peace, you find yourself being forced to take sides to prove your alliance and are called "disloyal" if you don't. Once the fight is over and the parties make up, you find yourself copping the blame and end up being made the scapegoat in all the mess.

Response

Stay out of the fray! Always try to stay out of matters that do not concern you. By all means, offer condolences or a shoulder to cry on when they need to, but if asked to take sides, ensure all the parties involved know you are not going to be drawn into their argument no matter how hard it may be. Draw a firm line as to where you stand and encourage the parties to seek professional advice if they are unable to resolve their issues alone.

The Apologizer

Do you always feel that you need to apologize for your actions, or those around you? When you finally get that promotion at work over your friend, you are made to feel guilty that your friend has missed out on the opportunity. When your friend does something to upset you, you will often find yourself making excuses for their actions and end up feeling responsible for making a big deal out of nothing. You cannot extract blame from yourself because your friends have always made you feel that you are responsible for everything that happens around you.

Response

Breathe! You are not responsible for everything that goes wrong in the world! If your friend cannot be happy for your successes, then you need to stop and ask yourself if there is a need for such a negative person in your life.

Everyone should be responsible for their own actions, and those who avoid taking responsibility are often those who still have a lot of growing up to do. If you feel upset at your friend's actions, let them know and tell them that you've been hurt by them. If they refuse to take responsibility for how they've made you feel, then perhaps it's a good time to start rethinking whether you have space for such an immature and selfish person in your life.

Last Word

No matter the type of friend you have, always follow through on what you say or promise by setting boundaries you are comfortable with, and by indicating the parameters within which you feel safe to conduct the friendship. If you fail to adhere to your initial boundaries, a great deal of confusion will develop, and your friends will not know what is acceptable and what to avoid. On the other hand, without the consistent reinforcement of your boundaries, people will begin to realize that anything goes, and very soon you may find yourself being ignored.

With firm boundaries in place, you are actively making a decision that you will allow yourself to be happy and respected, and that you are not reliant on others for happiness and security. If you are currently faced with a demanding friend who is selfish and egotistical, or if you have a friend who clings to you and demands your time and input at the expense of your own happiness and inner peace, then you need to start today to put those boundaries in place.

Remember, each person is a unique individual with their own ideas and personal idiosyncrasies. By showing your friends respect and by taking responsibility for your own actions without blaming anyone else, you demonstrate that you have a good, strong connection to your core values, and you are most comfortable with who you are and therefore not intimidated by others. Thus, you have solid personal boundaries in place, and you are seldom, if ever, coaxed into abandoning your values and boundaries for anyone else.

Always seek to communicate in an honest and open manner with others. Mutual respect for each other's thoughts and ideas are vital for the success of any friendship. Opt for discussing your expectations with your friends and hearing what they, too, expect from the alliance rather than presuming you know everything about them. Assumptions lead to a great deal of confusion and needless heartache. No matter how close your friendship may be, always ask for their opinions and participation, and in turn, always speak up of your own thoughts and feelings so that all parties are clear on the expectations of each other.

Chapter 4: Boundaries for Family

If you've never set boundaries with your family before, the idea of sitting down with them to broach the topic can be a challenging prospect. Where do you start? And, how strict should these boundaries be?

When you were young, you probably never even thought about setting boundaries because in many cases, these were already in place. You were most likely too oblivious to even recognize that you were acting well within the limits that were set upon you and, for the most part, just obeyed diligently.

Growing up, my siblings and I knew that to break a curfew or to arrive home after the promised time, was to bring the wrath of our father down on our heads. Strict, though he was, he treated us fairly and always gave us the opportunity to explain. However, at that time, his word was the law, and the boundaries my parents had instituted while we were growing up were clear and immovable.

The Influences at Home

It isn't uncommon to find children modelling the behavior of their parents or caregivers well into their adult years. When a child is nurtured in an environment with love and respect, you can be sure that these two values will drive very much how they act and what they expect in others. Similarly, if someone takes to muscling their way into relationships and try to take power from others, you may well be able to pinpoint this as a result of some kind of childhood trauma. Though not all behaviors will be directly linked to the experiences of your upbringing, the influences from your family are strong and can be deeply seated into the identity you have today.

Before you start setting boundaries with your family, have a think about the type of environment in which you grew up in. We may not be aware of how much influence our childhood and our memories of growing up have affected us, but our actions, feelings, emotions and everything we have around us can be shaped largely by our experiences that occur in our younger and formative years.

For example, if you are shy and timid and find that you cannot voice your opinions without feeling anxious and breaking out into a cold sweat each time, ask yourself, since when did you start feeling this way? Or, if you're the type who cannot stop putting your nose into other people's problems and can't help but gossip with those around you, think about what type of people you grew up around?

Your answers may or may not link back to your memories from home, but if they do, then these are the answers you may wish to start exploring when you start to go about setting boundaries for the people who have known you for maybe the longest time of your life.

Understanding the Relationship with your Parents

Your parents are the first people who know you and will often be the ones to have first introduced boundaries into your life.

"Yes, you can go out to the shops alone, but you must come back before 6pm."

"No, you cannot make friends with strangers just because they give you candy."

When we were younger, we would have simply taken these as instructions of what we could and could not do, and innocently played along. Now, we are able to recognize that simple instructions such as the above were only teaching us about safety and generosity, and that there are certain limits and restrictions to our freedom and our kindness that we needed to be aware of.

As we become adults, we may now find the need to redefine these boundaries to better suit the adult that we've become.

"Yes, I can go out alone and I can stay out late if I want to."

"Yes, I can make friends with strangers, if I feel safe around them"

The boundaries that we have with our parents, however, may not be that easy to redefine.

"You are my child so I should know everything about you."

"You're living under my roof, so you must listen to what I say."

You may find that the moment when you've finally grown up is when you first find the courage to stand up to your parents. Difficult though this may seem, standing up and asserting that you are now an adult and can think for yourself will liberate you and make you feel that you have matured as a person.

Some parents understand the fact that their kids have grown up, and they are happy to step aside and offer their support when they need to. Other parents have a hard time letting their children go, so they often become the "hoverers" in the new family structure. If this is the case, make sure the boundaries that you've set are clear to them, explain to them whey these boundaries are in place and why you feel so strongly for them. Don't fall prey to assuming that they will automatically understand your needs and expectations because you've spent a good portion of your life growing up before their eyes. If it requires many conversations for them to get the message, then by all means, make the time to do so.

It may come as a shock if someone such as a parent, who you have respected all your life, refuses to respect your boundaries especially if you've never questioned theirs when growing up. However, with parents, it's best to remind ourselves of the generation gap that ultimately separates us and treat any and all violations with patience and understanding.

Understanding the Relationship with your Siblings

Often the first "friends" you will have in life will be the siblings who have grown up with you. These are the people who have lived in the same household and under the same parents, and so would know all the struggles and successes you would have faced growing up.

You may have had a good relationship with your sibling when you were younger and may have grown up to have the relationship fall apart. Just like how you are no longer the same person that you were as a child, so too will your sibling undergo their own changes through life.

Sometimes this means that they may no longer feel like family, instead they may resemble a stranger.

For example, if you've moved out from home and only made a visit to your family after a good four years later, you may be shocked to see that your once teenage brother have already grown into an adult. You crave for the time that you've missed and so you do whatever you can to compensate the lost time by treating him to meals and the things that you have. However, you cannot ignore that he has changed into a completely different person and the small lectures that you used to give him without much concern have now become unacceptable. Struggling with this new dynamic that you have, you eventually realize that you need to relearn the relationship and not assume that the bond that you use to have has remained unchanged.

If you find that the sibling of yours is instead the one living in the past and hasn't matured over the years, then speaking your mind and showing your patience is key to supporting them and helping them grow with you. Don't forego all the good that you had with them just because they now cannot see eye-to-eye with you. The memories that you both share are precious, so afford them the effort that you have to work things out together.

Understanding Extended Family

Our relationships with our extended family can often be a tricky one. These are the people who we've had no part in choosing and may have no special bond with, and yet are often permanent fixtures in our lives. You may never know where you stand with these people because you may only see them during special occasions littered throughout the year, such as birthdays or Christmas parties, so you may not have had a chance to really get to know them. What you do know though is that you must respect these "aunts" and "uncles", and "in-laws", because they mean a great deal to those who mean a lot to you.

When an extended family member infringes on your boundaries, it can be tempting to just let it slide – after all, it's not like you'll see them until the next birthday party, which may be a good few months away. However, if you find yourself feeling this way, consider that perhaps you are not offering any respect to them, because you have not afforded them the opportunity to understand you and what you value.

Ask yourself if you know what their boundaries are with you. If you've answered somewhere along the lines of, "I don't know", then chances are they also don't know what your boundaries are. Try to find an opportunity to really get to know them properly by starting a conversation with them. In the case of an aunt who you may only have vague childhood memories of, it's never too late a time to remember that they are an individual with their own thoughts and feelings, and not just an identity that you've prematurely assigned, such as "that aunt who bakes the pumpkin pie for Thanksgiving".

When after trying to know them at an individual level, you still cannot establish any personal bonds with them, don't automatically feel that the issue is with you or them. Sometimes, we need to accept that we can't always get along with those around us but as long as we can keep a good, safe distance away, we can safeguard ourselves from any harm that may come our way.

Managing Boundary Violations from Family

A lot of the times, boundary violations from family members come with an unhealthy dose of guilt designed to make you feel bad about yourself and to retreat.

"How dare you speak to me like that, after everything I did to raise you!"

"You've changed! You weren't always like this when you were younger!"

It will be frustrating and can even be hurtful that the people you grew up respecting can treat your needs and wants as irrelevant or even secondary to how they feel. However, aggression only creates counter anger, so avoid this emotion at all costs. Remain focused but be kind and show the other your patience and understanding. It's difficult to challenge someone who is calm and kind. Perhaps, through mutual exchange of ideas, you may find the opportunity to compromise and in so doing, keep both parties happy. With kindness and a positive, calm approach, you may well win the other person over to your point of view.

Remain in Control

When you have your boundaries, you should have nothing to be ashamed of even if a disruptive family member tries to put in their two cents. By remaining in charge and taking ownership of your actions, boundaries, and values, what you are doing is reinforcing your control. When the family member who is at fault sees that you will not back down, your actions may cause them to think twice about their continued transgressions.

You could go all out and tell your parents to butt out of your life because you no longer need their advice. Or, you can take a more caring approach by telling them you are grateful for the grounding and support they gave you while you were growing up. You can thank them for teaching you the importance of having boundaries and then suggest that you are now ready to put all they've taught you into practice.

As soon as you are aware that your boundaries have been crossed, take control of the situation and face the perpetrator head-on. Make sure you stay calm as you inform them of your boundaries and that you do not enjoy their transgression. Be very explicit about what you expect and find out if the family member is willing to cooperate. When you make your expectations clear and concise, there can be no room or excuse for misunderstandings.

The most important fact to keep in mind is that you are now an adult, and as such, you are no longer a child who cannot think for themselves, despite whether your family sees you this way. Parents, siblings and other family members will always hold on to that young image of you because of the precious memories that you share. To break that image, allow them every opportunity to discover for themselves how you've grown and matured by demonstrating that you are quite capable of setting boundaries in your life, and sticking to these even in the face of conflict.

Enacting Consequences

When emotions are involved, it can be one of the most challenging situations to deal with. It will be difficult but avoid losing your cool in the middle of an argument and saying things you will later regret. Take time to think the matter through.

What was it that the family member did? Was the transgression intentional? Have I spoken to this person already about the importance of my boundaries? What was their initial response?

Based on your responses to these questions, you may wish to confront the family member before deciding on the most suitable consequences. Remember to remain firm but kind and polite during these dialogues, as you will want to avoid crushing anyone's ego or self-esteem. Avoid pointing an accusatory finger at the perpetrator and simply discuss how their actions made you feel and how it was a violation of an important boundary of yours. If the family member continues to ignore your boundaries and persist in transgressing these rules, then you need to demonstrate that you will not tolerate this by enacting out consequences.

Consequences are vital if you wish to reinforce the importance of the boundaries that have been crossed. If you have a partner in your life, then you will need to also discuss this with them, so that you are both on the same page from the get-go. You both need to decide on what consequences you believe will work for all family members, not just yours.

Maybe, you decide on a "no-speak" for a few days. This decision may work if you have kept in daily contact with your family members. If not, perhaps you can stop the Sunday family get-together at your home, or not attend this function if it is held elsewhere. Whatever your decision, stick to it and don't allow your emotions to waylay you. The bottom line is to ensure your family members understand your boundaries are important and that any attempts to disregard or disrespect them are inexcusable.

Don't Take Their Reactions to Heart

You may find your family responds negatively to your boundaries, or even try to convince you to remove them altogether. Their response may be due to their lack of understanding rather than their concerted effort to undermine your rules. This is in no way an excuse for their behavior, but it may help you understand where they are coming from. Whatever their point of view, remain steadfast in your resolve to have your boundaries respected by all members of the family.

If you become the brunt of future family jokes or members of the family may try to shame or blame you, so what? That's their prerogative, but it doesn't change the fact that your boundaries remain intact, no matter what. Don't take the negative reactions of the family to heart and ruin the rest of your life worrying about these people and how they feel about you. Provided you have done nothing to willfully harm your family members, you should be proud that you have stood your ground and shown that you will not tolerate their disrespect.

At some point, these people will start to realize that they need to take responsibility for their own actions. When, and if they do, they will discover it took a great deal of courage on your part to maintain your boundaries. Who knows, they may even commend you for your action when they've had a chance to reflect on things.

Good, open, authentic communication and unbiased dialogue forms the basis of any solid, lasting relationship. But, remember, communication is a two-way process. Therefore, expect your family members to bring their own boundaries into the discussion. Though this idea may sound daunting at first, by being open and honest with each other, you are given the opportunity to lay a solid, lasting foundation between all the family members. Sometimes, all it takes is just one brave person to set the tone for everyone else to follow.

Setting boundaries is a skill that requires a great deal of effort and consistent practice. Each time you fail, don't be disheartened. Use these opportunities to fine-tune your techniques. Over time, you will find your confidence improves, and soon, you will have mastered the skill of setting and refining your boundaries to suit each new stage of your life.

Seeking Support

Not every family member will adhere to your rules and respect your boundaries. However, just because some individuals can't understand your values or see from your point of view, there will be others who can, and will value and respect you for holding firm. These are the people to whom you should turn to in times of need for advice and support. They may be willing to offer you the help you need in dealing with the disrespectful family member who repeatedly tramples your boundaries with a total disregard for your feelings and values, so take the offer if it is available. If you have no one to run to from within the family, seek the support elsewhere. Perhaps a trusted friend or a colleague will be able to advise you or give you good suggestions on what to do or how to act that will curtail the advances of the unwanted family member.

If after multiple attempts, or if the advice you've received just doesn't seem to resolve the situation that you find yourself in, then now may be the time to seek professional support. Broken relationships don't heal themselves, so allow a professional, objective, outside approach to help you mend the relationship. It's important to remember that receiving professional help isn't a sign of weakness or that you have failed, but rather it demonstrates that you are self-aware and recognize that you alone cannot solve every problem that is out there.

In some cases, the offending family member may be asked to join a few of these sessions. If they refuse or fail to commit to this, it may be a good idea to start avoiding this person when you can. Any further engagement with this person may be misconstrued as you simply playing into their hand and they are likely to continue to try to force you to accept their demands again. Though this emotional battle of wills is both stressful and wearisome and is likely to leave you feeling despondent and anxious or maybe even angry, you need to remain firm in your values and respect yourself enough not to give in.

Don't feel obligated to accept an invitation to Thanksgiving at their home the next time it happens. There's little point in willingly exposing yourself to the negative reception you know awaits you, not to mention the snide little comments that will be made within earshot. While the difficulty with safeguarding your boundaries is particularly difficult when it comes to family members and relatives, always remember that there is no need for you to have to apologize for having boundaries and for setting standards by which you have chosen to live. Your family needs to come to terms with and treat you as an adult as an individual, and not just a child who was in their care, anymore.

Healthy Boundaries with Your Partner

Unlike your other family members, your relationship with your partner was a choice that you made, and so you should be confident that when establishing boundaries with this person, that they possess the ability to respect and compromise where necessary so as to allow the relationship to grow and strengthen.

Healthy boundaries are those that encourage people to understand their own feelings, thoughts, and behaviors in terms of how others around them think and feel. For example, a healthy boundary is to let your partner know the latest information about your personal life, including your friends and occurrences at work, and accept their suggestions while maintaining your integrity and privacy. What will breach this line and start heading into unhealthy territory, is if your partner begins to expect that their suggestions are taken on board, without allowing you to decide if it is the solution you want for yourself.

Healthy boundaries should be flexible as they change with time and circumstances. They should be open to suggestions and, in some instances, negotiation. Out of respect, healthy boundaries always take the other person's point of view into account.

Identifying Toxic Boundaries

If you find that your partner ignores the boundaries you've established in the relationship, then what that should indicate to you is that they are disrespecting the original rules that that you have both agreed to since the beginning of the relationship. Boundaries are of a different type of importance in an intimate relationship as parties can easily and unknowingly invade each other on a physical, emotional, and sexual level. The hurt that can come from these breaches can have a detrimental effect and impact on the longevity of a relationship.

When there are toxic or dangerous boundaries, then there is no possibility for negotiation. Any offer of support or suggestion might be turned down because such an offer is seen as an immediate threat to the structure. Toxic boundaries result in unhappy, poorly established relationships filled with constant disappointments, resentment, and lots of confusion. If you find yourself in this situation, you will realize that they suck up all your energy and drain your emotional resources without any positive returns.

Feeling lonely and unable to go about the business of living without your partner may mean you have not developed your independence. You may feel uncomfortable to attend a family function when your partner is away on a business trip because you feel insecure when you are on your own. You can't see yourself as an individual, but only as part of a couple because you have somehow lost track of your own identity by not knowing what it is that you can offer without the person present. When you feel you need to rely absolutely on another person for your happiness and security, it is a clear signal that your boundaries need to be sorted out now.

It may be that you have low self-esteem that encourages you to turn to others for recognition. Ask yourself if this has always been the case before you met your significant other. If this was a change that occurred only after being in the relationship with them, then you will need to figure out what actions or events have driven you to become this way. Is it because you no longer have autonomy over yourself and rely on your partner for physical and emotional needs? Or is it that your partner encourages your dependance on them in order to sustain the relationship?

When you begin to suspect that the boundaries that you have with your partner are fueling only toxic behavior and toxic emotions, then it's time that you reevaluate these boundaries together and be honest and open with each other. Afford the ability to make compromises to make things work, but as always if you find that your partner isn't willing to respect those important values that you hold, then you will need to reassess whether the relationship should continue for both parties involved.

Healthy Boundaries for Your Children

If you have children, it is essential that you set firm, consistent, healthy boundaries for them as soon as they are young. With good boundaries, your children are more likely to grow up to be well-disciplined, socially competent, and responsible adults.

How do busy parents, struggling to maintain their own boundaries, manage to teach their children healthy, positive boundaries? Below are the eight rules I always go by:

1. **Set a Good Example**

Your child learns by imitating your actions, words, and behavior patterns. Which is why it's important that as a parent, you pay attention to your own actions and responses to situations especially when around your children. When you treat your child and other family members with respect, you will be treated in a similar manner. By controlling your own behavior, you ensure you set a good example for your child.

2. Pay attention to Your Child

Even when they're left alone to play with their friends, make sure you keep an eye on how they are and how they behave around others. When you notice that they've acted in a way that is in breach of the boundaries that you have been preaching, you will then be given a chance to address it straight away. This way, your child will understand that even if it may seem like their parents aren't around, boundaries still apply.

3. Convey Clear Expectations

It is important that parents clearly and concisely convey their expectations to their child. Your child needs to develop a clear understanding of what you expect of them and what you value most in your relationship with them. Explain the importance of honesty, integrity, empathy, and respect not only in the family but also socially. Encourage your child to talk about their expectations of you, their friends, and the situations in which they find themselves in.

4. Encourage Good Communication

The more you encourage your child to communicate with you during their early years, the more open and cooperative they are likely to be as they grow up. Communication is a two-way process involving talking and listening attentively from both sides.

5. Learning the Importance of Consequences

It is important to ensure that your child understands that every action leads to consequences, whether negative or positive. Accountability is a value that teaches us to take responsibility for our actions and to be mindful of the fact that breaking rules brings upon negative consequences.

So, for example, if your child is disrespectful to you, they need to understand there will be consequences holding them accountable for their actions. Perhaps, send them to the "naughty corner", and only allow them to play with their toys once they apologize for breaking the rules that you have both agreed upon. Or, let them know that you won't buy them their favorite toy or item, because they did not respect the boundaries that have been set in place.

6. Joint Planning is Important

Joint planning can go a long way to ensuring your child accepts the home rules. The secret is to start early in your child's life with a few basic rules. Although they may be too young to participate fully in planning boundaries, explain in simple terms what you expect. As the child grows older, it is a great idea to bring them on board for family pow-wows when they too can have their say about planning the rules and regulations for family behavior.

7. Listen Respectfully

Remember to respectfully listen to your child and guide their thoughts and ideas without ever shouting them down or ignoring their contributions. Once the rules have been put in place, stand firm. Parents who waver and change their boundaries from day to day, cause huge confusion and resentment in their child. If no one knows where they are in the greater scheme of things, there's bound to be some negative fallout.

8. Don't Give Up

Nothing worthwhile can be achieved overnight. Expect glitches and many questions from your child. Avoid beating yourself up when things don't work out the first time around. If they don't grasp the importance of boundary setting, keep giving them opportunities to learn. Patient persistence will pay off in the end!

Last Word

Navigating around family will always be tricky with the myriad of dynamics that you'll need to make sense of. Despite these people being some of the closest people in the world to you, at some point, your life experiences will diverge from theirs and coming to terms with that in itself can be another challenge. Never assume that you will have their understanding and empathy no matter what stage you are in life. Being clear and honest with who you are or who you've become is critical to ensuring that the relationships that you have with your family members receives the sustenance that it requires.

Though you may not be able to choose the family you have grown up with, your bond with your life partner is different. Never subject yourself to accept less than what you are worth under the guise of love and making compromises. Though healthy boundaries should always be open to suggestions and constant reevaluations to reflect growth and positive changes in relationships, it should also make you feel safe and at peace with who you are and how you feel the relationship is going. The respect that you share for each other will allow your relationship to flourish, so that when it comes time to having children, you can both confidently pass your values onto them.

Chapter 5: Boundaries for Work

Why on earth are boundaries needed in the workplace? Don't you already work within specific boundaries governed by timelines, your work area, the number of projects you are busy with, not to mention the fact that you are at your boss' beck and call?

Having clear boundaries at work encourages efficiency and productivity, as well as affording you the luxury to take time off to rest to allow you to recharge your mind when you most need it. These days modern technology often encourages us to be on-the-job day in and day out, subjecting us to the ugly emotions of stress, anxiety and feelings of being burnt-out or over-worked. When you have the necessary boundaries in place, you maintain your mental, emotional and psychological health, which will offer clarity when you need it, thereby enabling you to excel in your work and improve in your career.

Successful People Set Boundaries

If you look to the most successful people in the world, they will all tell you that having boundaries at work is what will allow you that precious thing called, "work-life balance". Work-life balance occurs when there is harmony between your life at work and your life at home, and where this balance lends support and strength to each other.

Most working people spend the majority of their day either in the office or on work-related projects, and so will not be aware of how much their work life bleeds into their personal life. By setting the right kinds of boundaries, you are taking control to make sure that there is a clear distinction between the two.

Workplace boundaries that you need to consider in any environment include both physical and psychological boundaries. Physical boundaries are those barriers that relate to your personal physical work area as well as your personal space. Defining your workspace is vital if you are to complete tasks and meet deadlines without interruptions. This area and all your personal work equipment should be out of bounds to your coworkers. It's important to ensure that people know that they may not walk into your workspace unannounced and that nothing in the designated area belongs to them. These boundaries will hopefully protect you from the perpetual "borrowers" of stationery and the like. *Personal* physical boundaries include infringements of your personal physical self. These barriers protect you from the overly enthusiastic "hug-bunnies," hand-holders and shoulder-clutches, where a simple greeting or handshake will suffice.

Your mental and psychological boundaries are established when you interact with coworkers, accept instructions from your boss, or work cooperatively in a team situation. These boundaries pertain to your thoughts, ideas, and opinions in relation to your work environment. Leaders tend to have well-structured psychological boundaries in place, so that they won't be swayed in their opinions, especially when it affects outcomes and the performances of the staff that report to them.

Boundaries that protect your psychological space ensures that you don't waste time second guessing your boss or coworkers' motive every time that there are disagreements or a clash of opinions. Having good, solid psychological boundaries will allow you to avoid those who enjoy spreading dishonest rumors of you or those around you, so that you can focus on your work and get things done. You will also find that you won't be falling prey to the "manipulators" who act on jealousy or are out to inhibit or sabotage your work or chance of success.

Workplace Guidelines to Consider

To start structuring your boundaries at work, you need to clearly understand the environment that you are working in. By understanding the conditions of your employment, you will be better positioned to understanding what is required of you and your role in the company. Often times, feelings of stress, overwork and anxiety comes from not knowing what is expected of you, which naturally compels you to overcompensate with additional effort and commitment. By having a clear understanding of the contract you have signed, you offer no doubts or uncertainties to those who may wish to take advantage of you.

1. *Working Hours, Overtime, Leave, and Time Off*

Be sure you have a clear understanding of your working hours. This should include your daily start and end times. Included here, you should know how long tea/coffee and lunch breaks are.

Then you need to find out if the company has an overtime policy and how this works. Will you be expected to work overtime? What type of leave is allowed and when may this be taken? Is it paid or unpaid leave?

Ensure all these details are clearly noted in your contract or before you begin your role, and that you understand your responsibilities to the company. Also, be aware that you need to create boundaries in relation to how long you will work each day and whether or not you will do overtime. Ensure you make your boundaries very clear and that you will not compromise on these things.

2. *Office/Workspace*

Find out where you will be expected to work. Do you have an office or a cubicle? Is the office plan "open" and, if so, where will you be placed in relation to walk-through traffic, good lighting, fresh air, and potential noise-pollution?

Set clear boundaries about how you prefer to work and that interruptions during your day will not be encouraged. If unnecessary noise disturbance is not something you enjoy, let your co-workers know by way of not engaging in the chats, and only allow yourself social chats to take place during breaks instead.

3. Amenities

Do you have access to a canteen, library, fitness gym, outdoor area, cloakroom with shower facilities? Will you have a personal locker or be expected to store personal items, such as your gym kit, in your office space?

Ensure you are aware that your privacy and safety is assured at all times when you use the amenities and/or gym equipment.

4. To whom are you responsible?

Make sure you understand the line of command and identify the boss/bosses and any other senior managers and colleagues.

From the get-go, establish a professional relationship with your senior co-workers and never feel the need to compromise this relationship. Maintain a polite, well-mannered distance and ensure everyone understands your work ethics.

5. Is anyone responsible to you?

Is there anyone on the corporate ladder below you for whom you are responsible? The same boundaries will apply there as above. Only, you will need to set the standard you expect from your junior co-workers.

6. Work Functions, Private Details, and Dating

Are you expected to attend all work functions including seminars, discussions, and the like? What about team-building events? Should you attend social functions alone or with a partner?

Make your boundaries clear with reference to your willingness or unwillingness to fraternize with staff and to maintain a professional distance at all times. Whatever the decision, ensure that your private number and details are not up for public knowledge and that work-related matters will be dealt with during working hours only.

Remember that any worthwhile organization that is governed by sensible, realistic rules and boundaries generally thrives and grows. You may be familiar with, or have previously signed, a Code of Conduct, which contain the rules and regulations that govern how staff should behave in and amongst the workplace. Make sure that this Code of Conduct aligns to your values and that you feel safe and respected, knowing that you have your workplace's support in addition to the boundaries that safeguard you.

Communicate your Concerns

No matter how challenging it may be, always remember to discuss your limits clearly and succinctly. For example, if you don't want coworkers to contact you after hours, tell them this firmly but respectfully. Inform them that you will only be available in case of an emergency, and make sure to then discuss what constitutes an emergency with clear examples.

Clear, concise communication of your boundaries to your coworkers allows them to understand your limits as well as your expectations. Communication is a vital thread that should run through all your relationships from your personal and family bonds, to your social and professional ties.

In case of a boundary violation, be brave enough to deal with this incident as soon as practicable. Every day that you ignore these violations or pretend they never occurred, the memory of it and the indignation you feel will torment you until you have an emotional blowout. The sooner you bring the matter out into the open, the quicker it can be resolved and the stronger the message you send out about keeping your boundaries intact.

For example, if you are asked to take sides in a work-related matter in which one coworker has a difference of opinion with another, tell them clearly and politely that you are not interested in taking sides, and that the matter in question does not concern you. Challenging though this type of response may sound, it's always best not to be drawn into matters of this nature as it may interfere with your line of work, or have you embroiled in affairs that are most likely irrelevant to your work life.

Set Structure In your Day

You may find it useful to always work to an agenda. Whether you have a meeting with the boss, your coworkers or clients, draw up a plan of action and stick to it. Make a note of the start and end times as well as the topics to be raised. Not only does this make you look more professional, but it also saves time and everyone else knows where you stand in the greater scheme of things.

For example, if your coworker continues to interrupt you throughout the day, with questions and requests for help, suggest a brief morning meeting of around 10 minutes during which they can raise all their queries. Ensure they understand you are not up for any more disruptions during the day that is outside of this time. Your coworkers are less likely to interrupt you during your workday when you have clearly established times of when you do not wish to be disturbed.

You may find making quick notes of these brief meetings will also help your coworker to stay on track. Prioritize tasks and stick to your program. Tackle one task at a time and work it through to its completion before considering the next job. Ensure that your boundaries are realistic and well established. Once people learn what is acceptable and what you will not tolerate, they are likely to work more effectively with you.

Keep Your Personal Life Separate

As we've mentioned, it's important to set yourself clear boundaries at home in respect to work-related matters. Plan a specific time to check emails and answer those that are important, before turning off your devices in order to enjoy quality family time or "me-time". Go completely offline on your days or weekends off. This will give you a much-needed opportunity to replenish your reserves.

During working hours, if you have made an error or have failed to complete a task on time, be honest and own up to the mistake. Don't beat around the bush, instead be upfront when your boss requests for an explanation as to why you are behind schedule. Even if the reason is due to issues at home, try an answer like, "I haven't yet completed job A, but I'm working on it now and hope to present it to you by X time." No one is interested in your home affairs when there are deadlines that need to be met, especially the person who has hired you do the job. If you feel the need to discuss your personal situation, reserve this for when you are on your lunch break, or after work drinks, when work is no longer in the picture.

Similarly, if it is your coworkers who haven't completed their part in the project, don't allow them to distract you with outside drama and remain focused on the task at hand. You don't want to fall into a situation where you end up taking the blame for your coworker's mistakes simply because you were too enthralled in their riveting stories of their ex, or their botched kitchen renovations!

Keeping it professional and not letting everyone know about your personal life when dealing with your work will garner you respect from your boss as well as your peers.

Know Your Coworkers and the Resources Available

Getting a good feel for your coworkers' expectations and what they are willing to tolerate, will give you an idea of where to start with your own boundaries. Just remember that your standards for quality work do not need to be compromised or sacrificed by anyone.

Learning to delegate tasks is a great way to share the workload and ensure tasks are completed in a timely manner. When you can share the workload successfully, you will avoid the feeling of being overwhelmed and submerged in insignificant tasks that take up too much of your time. When you have a good team in place and can assign various tasks to them, it allows you peace of mind where you can escape for a few hours knowing the job will continue to run without you. If you are in a leadership role, learn to allocate tasks that do not require your attention to someone else with the expertise to carry these tasks out instead. Being able to delegate tasks appropriately is a great skill that will ensure you will not be pushed to your limits and crash as a result of taking on too much.

Technology can be enormously helpful in setting up boundaries. There are a variety of tools that you can use to set dates and reminders, schedule meetings, and notify customers of developments and delivery times. If you can take a short vacation, technology can be programmed to stand in for you, take messages and only pass the most important information onto you. In this way, you can remain updated even while you are on leave.

When you are approached to take on an extra duty, try to avoid the 'knee-jerk' reaction to say yes. Rather, take a moment to consider the question or instruction and decide how best to tackle it. By pausing, you allow yourself space to breathe and to make a less emotive response. Saying "no" may become a realistic option when you have that extra time to think things through.

When you walk out of your office at the end of every busy day, switch your mind off along with all the technical devices in your workspace. If this is too challenging for you, then allow yourself to routinely check work-related devices only once after you have left the office for the day, and no more.

It is never healthy to take on more than you know you can handle. In the end, a job well done will win hands down over a partially completed mess. This is why you should make sure to take some time off from work. Use your sick days as well as family responsibility leave. If this leave is due, using it will help you avoid ending up a physical or mental wreck from lack of rest.

Don't think that you are alone in the battles that you take to the workplace. By recognizing the number of resources that you have around you, boundary setting will become much easier.

Prepare for Infringements

Goodness! This sounds as though potential violations are gathering on your threshold!

However, forewarned is forearmed, as the saying goes. Visualize potential transgressions of your boundaries and decide beforehand what the consequences will be to the perpetrators. This way, you don't leave anything to chance.

So, imagine a senior colleague mails you on the weekend with some important work that needs to be completed by Monday. Will you take on the job, or politely decline? Will you offer to go into the office earlier on Monday to process the request, or will you be pressured into sacrificing precious family time to complete the task at home?

If you are unsure of your decision, have a think about whether this is a repeat offender. If so, see if you can pinpoint when the boundary was infringed upon and whether you had made any efforts to reinforce your boundaries with them. If not, take the opportunity now to do so, so that you won't have to face these scenarios again in the future.

By thinking scenarios through in your head, you are unlikely to be caught off guard and you can respond as planned. Despite your best efforts, not everyone will understand, let alone respect, your boundaries. There will also be those coworkers who do not agree with your boundaries and still others who will view these barriers as a personal rebuff. Whatever the case, stick to your resolve out of self-respect, if nothing else.

Final Word

Building boundaries is a skill that takes patience, time, and lots of practice. If, after all your efforts, your work environment remains toxic and your boundaries continue to be disregarded, it's time to move on. By trying to stick the job out, your health, happiness, and emotional stability will only be compromised and leave you unhappy and stressed out. Your workplace should afford you peace and an opportunity for growth. If neither of these things are present, know your worth and start looking elsewhere the next chance you get!

Chapter 6: Boundaries for *You*

When we talk about setting boundaries for ourselves, what we're really talking about is the idea of self-care. Self-care encompasses all that you consciously do to ensure your mental, physical, and emotional health and well-being are in good balance. It encourages you to perpetuate a good, healthy relationship with yourself that ultimately builds a positive self-image and enables you to interact in a confident and constructive manner with others around you.

Unfortunately, self-care is all too often one of those areas you may neglect due to being inundated with work and responsibilities that you feel need your immediate attention. Sadly, many of us react to stressful work situations in much the same way. We generally put everyone and everything else before our own needs. It often takes a serious jolt in the form of sudden ill health or burnout, to call us back to acknowledging that self-care is of paramount importance to our emotional, mental, and physical well-being.

All About Self Care

A good starting point for self-care is to realize your self-worth. Learning to love and respect yourself enables you to build a healthy relationship with yourself. Knowing your value also reminds you that your needs are as important as those of other people. When you practice good self-care habits, everyone in your orbit benefits from your positive vibes.

Self-care is also about maintaining a healthy work-life balance. Overworking, or attempting to multitask do little more than increase your stress levels and create a decidedly dangerous imbalance in your life. Hypertension, exhaustion, and insomnia often follow when you fail to take care of your health needs. Productivity begins to fail too, when you neglect self-care.

By deciding to live your life to the fullest instead of simply existing is yet another way in which you can practice self-care. Despite the many responsibilities you have to your family, friends, home, and work, your chief responsibility should be to yourself. You might think that it's selfish to do so, but it's not. Your importance to others cannot be easily measured but, without you, they would find life unbelievably challenging. So, self-care not only validates your value to yourself, but to others as well. Only when you are happy and healthy can you truly be there for anyone else.

Explore New Hobbies

Practice self-care by taking up a new hobby such as painting or writing. You may decide to invest time and energy in an exciting new venture like hiking, mountain climbing, or figure skating. When you take a break from the mundane chores, you allow yourself precious time to renew and uplift your spirits. These activities enrich your life and rejuvenate you while also acting as de-stressing mechanisms.

Self-care and managing stress also involve good eating habits, regular exercise, and good sleep routines, all of which are vital for your continued health and well-being. Prepare to spend a little more time on these areas in your life. Avoid sleep deprivation at all costs as the lack of restful sleep degrades your mental capacity, physical stamina, as well as your emotional stability.

Instead of grabbing that cup of coffee as you dash off to work each morning, consider preparing a light, nutritious snack the night before so that you can grab it from the refrigerator as you head out of the door the next morning. Try to use every opportunity to walk rather than travel by car or taxi. Avoid the elevator and take the stairs, which is tantamount to a good, short run to build on your cardiovascular system.

Guard Your Personal Boundaries

One of the most important things you can do for yourself is to guard your personal boundaries without feeling guilty. Your safety, happiness, and inner peace are of great importance to your well-being, so don't undercut yourself when it comes to protecting what you value. Find a way to develop healthy personal boundaries that will enable you to cherish and value your own opinion, understand and accept your needs before those of others, interact positively yet appropriately with other people, all the while allowing you to accept and acknowledge other people's boundaries.

Setting boundaries to protect yourself and your interests are both a duty and responsibility.

People with boundaries are not only safe to be around but are often respected by others because everyone knows where they stand.

Challenging though it may be, good self-care comes with learning to turn people down and to not accept their advances or take on any of their burdens. Walking away, instead of being drawn into an unwanted situation, allows you time to gather your thoughts and reassemble your plan of action. All-in-all, saying "no" affords you more time to pursue those interests that bring you pleasure and inner peace.

For many of us who are natural 'pleasers,' our boundaries may not yet be firm enough to allow us to disagree when asked to participate in an activity or to simply say "no" when we should. If you are caught in a corner by your boss, a friend or even a family member, a good noncommittal answer can be, "I need time to consider your request. However, if you expect an immediate answer, it will have to be no."

Janet

Janet was just such a person who hated to disappoint others. She was always willing to help everyone in every way she could even though her offers of support exhausted her and often made it impossible for her to complete her own tasks on time.

After accepting to do a specific task that Janet admitted made her feel uncomfortable, she realized she had not taken heed of her intuition. She knew in her heart that this time she had taken on far more than she could handle. Instead of being positive and upbeat about the task as was Janet's usual nature, she fell into despair and found herself becoming angry and despondent.

A senior coworker noticed Janet's change of attitude and approached her to find out what had transpired to cause this paradigm shift in Janet's behavior. Janet explained that she was angry and disillusioned with herself because, despite her inner warnings, she never could say no to anyone. Helping others made Janet feel better about herself, and somehow more worthy as a person.

Because she always felt responsible for everyone else, Janet inflicted pain, unwanted stress, and anxiety on herself by not being able to put her own needs before those of others. Tracing these emotions back to her childhood, her therapist discussed ways to help Janet to overcome these feelings and to learn to stand up for herself again.

Breaking the habit as a person always needing to please others takes time and a reassessment of your boundaries. By ensuring your personal boundaries are well-structured and firm, you have the tools to set yourself up as a stronger person, who is empowered to stand up for your own interests. Taking a firm stand signals to others that you are not a walkover which, in turn, improves your chances for good self-care.

Give Yourself a Break

Although you may find it difficult, learning to make time for yourself is one way to practice self-care but taking time off is another great way of allowing yourself breathing space to regroup and relax. Spend weekends and holidays with family and friends. Travel and visit those exotic destinations you dream of! Time is a precious commodity that is all too soon gone, so use it well while you can. And, strange though it may seem, life will return to its normal hustle and bustle when you get back into the swing of things after your much-needed break.

Focus on the positives in your life. Everyone faces challenges in all sorts of ways, but it is how you decide to tackle these difficulties that makes the difference between good self-care and self-degradation.

Cherish the happy memories and faithful friendships, admire and appreciate the beauty around you, show gratitude for every small gift of time that people share with you, or the smile they give you each time you meet, the caring touch from someone who loves you, or the opportunity to hold the hand of an aged parent or a small child. There are so many small, sometimes overlooked opportunities to cherish that we can so quickly miss if we fail to stay focused on caring for ourselves.

Self-care is increased dramatically when you take time to be still and focus on your inner being. Regular mindful meditation offers you the opportunity to recharge your batteries, refocus your energies, pour out all the negative vibes you have inadvertently absorbed during the day and replace these with a quiet, calm, and peaceful inner self.

Physical Boundaries to Ensure Self-Care

Your personal boundaries offer support for self-care in that they preserve your space, protect your rights, and ensure your safety. These barriers keep you safe from physical harm as well as from infringements by other people who want to invade your space by getting closer than that you are comfortable. By ensuring you have good, clear, easily communicated physical boundaries in place, you increase your chances of protecting yourself from people who invade your personal space without invitation or overstaying their welcome. Infringements of these boundaries will only increase your stress levels, creating unwanted unpleasantness that may eventually lead to a decline in your overall health and well-being.

Being able to separate your feelings from those of the people with whom you live and work is vitally important to your self-care. Creating healthy boundaries at home, socially, and in your workplace encourages better self-esteem, less stress and anxiety, as well as creating a definitive line between yourself and others. Good self-care will empower you to avoid becoming entangled in emotional turmoil, thus strengthening your resilience against being unduly affected by other people's dramas.

Your sexual and emotional boundaries are closely linked. Mutual respect and understanding of your personal sexual boundaries are of paramount importance in an intimate relationship. They govern how you behave towards your partner and the way in which you view increased intimacy. Violations of these boundaries occur when you are subjected to unwanted sexual advances, leering, unwanted intimate touching, or coercion to embark on any sexual act that you do not want to participate in. In order to ensure good self-care, these intimate boundaries must be very clearly defined.

Then there are your material boundaries which include your possessions and wealth. They may limit your spending and govern your plans to maximize your savings. Violations occur when someone steals or damages your property or tries to force you to share your assets or belongings against your will. For example, a family member may borrow your car without your knowledge or permission. Practicing good self-care in this area of your life will likely ensure others have fewer opportunities to infringe upon your material boundaries.

There will always be that one person who constantly drains your resources for money, often with empty promises of paying you back as soon as they can. Try telling them that although you care for them, you won't be lending them any more money as they should start learning to take responsibility for themselves. Whatever situation you face, it is important that you remain steadfast in your decision to set firm boundaries to protect yourself against further abuse. In this way, you ensure good self-care.

Time is a valuable and all too transient asset, the importance of which is often overlooked. Most people feel they have too little time to achieve all they would like to attain. Set up well-defined boundaries for when people can visit or call you, especially during working hours. Family members often feel they have the right to drop in unannounced, so it is important to ensure these people are made aware of your time boundaries at home.

Healthy time boundaries entail ensuring you have sufficient time to pursue your own interests outside of work and the family, without endangering the time needs in other facets of your life. They also govern the number of hours you spend in front of the television, not working past a certain time, and when you get up each morning.

Time boundaries are breached when someone takes up too much of your time without due regard to your needs and wishes. An example of a time boundary violation is the coworker who hangs around your desk during the day, interfering with your opportunity to get work done.

One of the greatest values of self-care is to ensure you use some of your time for your own benefit in order to relax, recharge, and refocus.

The Benefits of Self-Care and Stress Management

You are more than likely juggling many responsibilities that you find challenging. While you may have accepted these obligations, willingly or otherwise, you now feel trapped under the weight of all these duties for which you believe you are solely accountable. The result is likely to be a severe case of burnout, unless you recognize the importance of immediately taking care of yourself.

The benefits of self-care are numerous and lasting when these are considered as an important part of your daily health regime. The ways in which each of us handles the stress in our lives will directly impact our ultimate success, well-being, inner peace, and happiness. It therefore behooves you to be aware of your needs before those of others in order to prepare and strengthen yourself to adequately cope with your responsibilities. By maintaining a healthy, regular self-care routine, you will discover the benefits in every area of your life.

Taking care of your physical health and well-being includes a well-balanced diet, a regular eating schedule, sufficient restful sleep, and plenty of healthy exercise. Together these benefits promote optimal body and brain function that ensure you are always at the forefront of your life's game.

People who practice good self-care are more capable of showing support for others because they have sufficient energy and the capacity to share their inner resources. Being constantly exhausted creates huge challenges for mothers in particular, who often try to balance on the fine line between holding down a job and keeping the family happy. With improved stamina, you have the advantage of ensuring you maintain good quality self-care.

By taking the time to rejuvenate yourself, you indicate to others that your needs are just as important as their own. Self-care promotes a positive self-esteem coupled with improved confidence - when you look good, you feel good about yourself and learn to value yourself accordingly. Increased energy levels afford you the opportunity to remain alert and focused. You have the advantage to stay ahead of the rest of pack while enjoying the benefits of your healthy self-care regime.

Practicing self-care routines empowers you to develop your creativity as well as your ability to function at your optimum mental capacity. When your body and mind are stressed it is difficult to complete tasks in a timely manner. Your productivity is also likely to be compromised resulting in increased frustration, and a distinct decline in your feelings of self-worth.

By ensuring you take care of your well-being you afford yourself the chance to be well-organized and as prepared as possible for challenges that every day brings. With a good, healthy self-care program in place, you are less likely to fall to pieces when your child spills their juice, or your car runs out of fuel. That is, when you enjoy sufficient good-quality rest and a healthy diet, your body and mind are well-prepared for most of the daily battles you may be called on to face.

Self-care projects are those that can give you the chance to enjoy a brief period alone, when you can just chill and "zone out" for a while. A visit to the spa, having a soothing massage, the opportunity to quietly meditate, or the chance to participate in a Tai Chi or dance class are all great opportunities for personal stress relief. Whatever your choice for stress relief might be, this is the time for relaxation and rejuvenation that you should not forgo.

Self-Care Tactics That Really Work

Just as soon as you realize you are in need of self-care, make every effort to set aside special time to indulge yourself. There are many ways in which you can enjoy the much needed "time out" to pamper yourself and rejuvenate your self-esteem, your mind, body and soul. Any of the suggested fail-proof, self-care strategies included here will go a long way to uplifting your spirits and improving your inner peace and well-being.

1. Enjoy a long, relaxing, fragrant bath while listening to your favorite music

2. Set time to enjoy a hobby that is away from the hustle and bustle of life, one that is close to nature, such as hiking, fishing, surfing or even a long drive

3. Treat yourself regularly to something you love, whether that be a bit of shopping or some time on the Play Station. However, make sure you set limits on this time so that you don't go on an unnecessary binge!

4. Visit a spa once a month for the full head-to-toe massage and all the delightful relaxing added trimmings that include health drinks and snacks, soft music, a relaxing swim in a heated pool or a refreshing bath filled with bubbles and fragrant petals.

When you have firm personal boundaries, you have increased self-respect and self-esteem.

You only give away what you want to share with whom you really trust, instead of allowing people to take what they want from you.

During your younger years, you were probably taught to share, so it is only natural to feel obligated to keep giving to people who ask you for support. Challenging though it may be to take a firm stand on sharing your wealth and belongings, it's better to make informed decisions about being charitable without feeling coerced to constantly give to needy people.

Your boundaries keep you safe and allow you to grow and develop as circumstances change. They govern your behavior and ensure other people treat you as you deserve to be treated. By being in tune with your needs, you are more likely to recognize opportunities for self-growth that will imbue your life with pleasure and inner peace.

Self-care involves making sure you never miss a step. Monitor your progress toward your goal while ensuring that you maintain good care of your own interests and well-being. By keeping yourself updated on every nuance and opportunity of your journey, you empower yourself to schedule time not only for new developments but also for self-care projects.

Good boundaries require honesty, integrity, and good communication. You can act in a firm, direct manner with people who in turn are more likely to respect you. People are often more respectful of you when they understand where they stand with you. Your boundaries create not only a safety net around you, but effectively keep other people in their place.

Norma

Norma ran a small education center where she tutored children with learning challenges after school. Though her business ran smoothly, she required the help of an accountant to relieve her of the added duty of keeping the financials updated. An old friend recommended Bradley, the person who did their company's books.

Norma and Bradley worked well together. Besides both being entrepreneurs, they both shared a love for animals, in particular Dachshunds. Between them, they had seven of these feisty, busy, little dogs.

Two years after they began working together, Bradley's lease came up for renewal. He asked Norma if he could board with her in her four-bedroom house, as it would be easier for him to work from there, and he felt the plan would work out well for them both.

Norma discussed her personal boundaries with Bradley, who agreed to respect these. Everything went smoothly for several months until Norma realized that certain personal possessions in her bedroom had been moved. After further investigation, she discovered documents were no longer in their respective place in her study and a substantial amount of money had disappeared from the safe. Instead of addressing these matters immediately, Norma let them slide on the pretext that she felt embarrassed, not to mention a little afraid to raise these issues with Bradley.

Gradually, Bradley began to find fault with Norma. He made snide remarks about her that caused her to feel insecure and uncomfortable. After she had spoken to a friend, Norma knew she had to take a stand, soon, if she were to get the situation under control.

Norma's concern reached its peak one day when she arrived home earlier than usual to discover Bradly agitated and unable to meet her eye when she greeted him. Upon entering her study, she discovered her computer was warm, so she knew the device had been recently used. She discovered someone had tried to access her personal bank account.

Norma decided to challenge Bradley. She reminded him of how he agreed to respect her boundaries and asked him what was going on. Bradley's angry response took Norma by surprise. He pushed her in what he would later describe, "frustration". Stunned by his actions, she couldn't quite register what was happening.

The following day, though Bradley was full of apologies and excuses for his behavior, Norma told him to leave. She explained that she had offered him a safe place to live, and he had overstepped her boundaries in a number of ways. Unfortunately, the abuse that erupted at this meeting resulted in Norma being hospitalized, and Bradley was later arrested for battery and assault.

Many months later, Norma confided that she had suspected something was "off" because Bradley kept trying to touch or hug her. He would unexpectedly appear on her side of the house after working hours, wanting to discuss a query he had with an account or talk about his dogs.

Norma subsequently discovered Bradley had never paid his share of the rent and had "borrowed" a great deal of money from the petty cash. She realized that the trust she had placed in Bradley to handle the financial affairs of her small business had backfired, leaving her in dire financial straits.

This experience affected Norma greatly, and so she decided to take some time away to allow herself to reevaluate her boundaries and reassess how she has been using these boundaries up until this point in her life. Whilst she had been able to establish her boundaries early in the relationship with Bradley, she found that she was guilty of not adhering to her own rules and letting things slide, even against her own intuition just so she could avoid confrontation. The time away allowed her to reflect on her life's progress and allowed her to make the changes she needed to be able to trust others again.

Today, Norma is a successful businessperson who takes responsibility for ensuring she maintains firm boundaries in every area of her life. Her employees enjoy working for her and find her strict adherence to the rules quite refreshing. Said one employee, "We all know exactly where we stand with Norma. If there's a problem, we discuss it immediately so that we can all move on in a more productive manner."

Norma has also realized the importance of self-care. Not only does she take regular breaks from work, but she insists that every employee takes an afternoon off once a month for just such a self-care treat. Fortunately, there is a wonderful spa and health and fitness on the roof in the same building. The upshot of this self-care compulsory regime is that all the employees and managerial staff have a positive, relaxed approach to their work. Productivity has increased and the number of workers suffering from stress related problems has dropped to almost zero. The knock-on effect for all the workers families has been just as positive.

Don't allow yourself to go through what Norma did to learn just how important boundary-setting and self-care is. Despite her later success, the stress and anxiety Norma endured during her recovery years would be something that she is only too keen to forget.

Chapter 7: Mutual Give and Take

We may all have been guilty to have assumed others' boundaries before, simply because our experiences in life can compel us to apply our learnings in scenarios that we find familiar. While you may know a great deal about your friend's life, you may have no idea about the depth and breadth of their boundaries unless you have a good and honest chat about it with them.

Being able to discuss your boundaries with your close friends and family will ensure they are aware of what you expect and what you will tolerate. By the same token, your family and friends will more than likely share their expectations of their boundaries with you. During these open, interactive discussions, it's easier to understand each other and to learn about each person's individual limits.

You should now be aware that our boundaries are often formed during our childhood through interaction with our family, friends, and environment. These barriers help to define who we are and to develop our sense of self-worth. They enable us to realize that though we are part of a family, we are separate people in our own right. Gradually, as we mature, we learn to characterize ourselves in terms of these boundaries.

While it is important to have your personal boundaries in place, it is vital that you recognize other people have boundaries as well. Well-defined boundaries, therefore, not only determine how we would like to be treated but also how we should treat others. The challenge arises in being consistent with the boundaries you have in place. Boundaries allow you to interact with different people in different ways without losing yourself somewhere in the process. That is, the boundaries you have with your partner may not be the same for your coworkers, but these boundaries should not compromise your values, nor your identity and sense of who you are.

Steps to Take Toward Being Respectful

Boundaries set the parameters for everyone in a relationship. Whether these be emotional, physical or intellectual boundaries, they ensure that all parties interacting in the relationship are entitled to the same respect. That is why having respect for each other is critical in all successful relationships in order for them to flourish and grow.

Boundaries are acutely personal and are closely linked to your needs and rights. Your personal needs are confirmed by your values and shaped by your culture. Your personality as well as your family beliefs, and your life experiences, all mold your boundaries. Just as each of us is unique and special in our own right, our boundaries will differ accordingly.

Respecting others means to listen and to discuss matters seriously when one party is in breach of the other's boundary line. When an outcome is reached, it is important that you stick by your end of the bargain, and also set expectations that the other do so, too. This way, you are both able to grow and mature together, so as to effectively strengthen the health of the relationship.

Learning to Read Others

Being able to identify certain aspects of the other person's behavior and attitude towards you can be beneficial in learning suitable ways of handling relationships successfully.

Verbal language as we know it, includes both spoken and written communication, with the tone or inflection of a person's words in a conversation being equally important. For example, if someone says, "I need help", you would expect that what they want is someone's assistance. But if they say this in between laughter, you may begin to suspect that it was a joke and not said seriously.

Tone can be tricky to capture in text messages and emails. In both instances, you will realize that the choice of words being used is deliberate and with an intended purpose.

Words are powerful – they can change one's mood, ruin one's character, and even drive one to suicide. This is why the words we choose to use must be carefully selected. When applying this to others, it means that we are best to take someone's words seriously and assume its literal meaning than to overthink it.

If someone keeps telling you to leave them alone, don't think that there's a hidden message in there, and really take that step back from them. If it is meant in jest, allow them to tell you, "that was a joke", instead of assuming one. When dealing with other people's boundaries, you are best to err on the side of caution, as there is no fun in running the risk of crossing their boundary line and making them feel uncomfortable.

Body Language

More powerful than the spoken word, a person's body language tells you a great deal about how they feel. If you take a good look at how the person presents themselves to you and to others, you may notice a subtle change in their stance or the movement of their body when they approach you. Facial expression can be a dead give-away as to how a person feels unless, of course, they are skilled in keeping their emotions under wraps.

So, let's that a look at a person who constantly finds fault with you. Do they do this in a playful, joking manner with a wide smile on their face? Are they arrogant and condescending when they speak to you? Do they lean towards you or away from you when they talk to you, or do they turn away when they address you?

Does the person hold eye contact with you or look away from you? Do they address you while they are talking to someone else? By interpreting all these physical signals, you will have a better understanding of the seriousness of the person's attitude toward you.

A common mistake that people make with reading body language is that they assume that the reaction that they see is a direct reflection of what is occurring. Take the example of you enjoying a conversation with a colleague at work, but at the same time some stressful matters at home keep playing on your mind. You may not be aware that a slight grimace from a wayward thought would present itself, but your colleague may see this and interpret it as a dislike of the conversation you two are having.

This kind of misunderstanding happens more often than you would think. And if the colleague doesn't bring it up you will never know that it had happened. This is why it's so important to not judge someone's body language towards you from just one incident. If you have the opportunity to interpret their body language in multiple settings, you can then be more confident that you are reading them correctly.

Recognizing Boundary Violations

Violations of boundaries come in different forms. Each of those mentioned here range from the most serious and consciously planned violations to the least intrusive yet still offensive types.

Violations may be aggressive in nature. These will include acts in which you vindictively damage the other person's property, physically abuse them by punching, kicking or hitting them. They could also include you exerting control over them in some way by refusing your child financial support, for example. Passive-aggressive violations occur when you interrupt someone, turn a cold shoulder or pointedly ignore, or gossip about them.

Accidental boundary violations often occur when you inadvertently bump into someone as you enter an elevator as the other person steps out of it. These violations can also occur when you touch someone's outstretched hand without intention to, or when reaching simultaneously for an object.

Trust in Your Intuition

Being self-aware involves in-depth knowledge of who you are as a person. Being intuitively aware of the other person with whom you have connected with enables you to determine how best to structure your boundaries while you take cognizance of theirs.

Your boundaries help to protect your basic human rights to say "no" without guilt, to be treated with respect, to have your needs acknowledged as being as important as those of others, and to have the right not to be forced to meet other's unrealistic expectations. We've spent a lot of time in this book, talking about just that. The very same holds true for the boundaries that other people have put in place.

Rely on your instincts not only to protect you but to also alert you to the feelings and fears of others. Most people have an inner awareness of when things are going wrong. This instinctive awareness acts as a protection in potentially harmful situations. In many cases, our instincts work well and are a reliable source of information. When you take note of these feelings you inadvertently avoid the development of unnecessary and often unpleasant drama, stress, and potential fear.

Ensure that you notify others of your boundaries in terms of "I" statements that leave no room for misinterpretation. "I'm happy to meet with you, but I'm not ready for an intimate relationship."

Value Yourself

Be proud of yourself and stand firmly by your boundaries without feeling in any way that these minimize your value. It is not only young people who fall prey to vacillation between maintaining and ditching their boundaries in order to please other people.

There is no need for you to feel you have to apologize for your boundaries, which are founded on the values you hold dear. If people don't like you for who you are, then there is little point in pursuing the relationship. By adhering to what you believe is best for you, you reinvest in yourself, adding value to the wonderful person you already are.

Respect the Other Person's Decision

As much as you expect your boundaries and decisions to be respected, you need to know that the same approach applies to your friends, family members and coworkers. So, before you put both feet in where they are not wanted, request permission from the other person to be in their space such as their office, or workroom. Respectfully and politely ask if they have a few minutes to chat, or if they can assist you with a specific problem. Barging in on them is likely to cause them to either instantly dislike you or to be unwilling to offer you their help.

Remember too, that their boundaries are probably in no way similar to yours, so don't assume that they are. If you are turned down verbally or by an action, respect the decision and back off.

Mutual honoring of each other's personal boundaries is vital for maintaining good relationships. As there is no neon sign indicating how someone feels or if you are transgressing their boundaries, you need to develop a keen awareness of the non-verbal clues that are often used to show a person's displeasure, fear, or confusion about your actions.

Learn to be observant and sensitive to the non-verbal clues people give out when they are with you. For example, when you meet someone, do they step back when you move forward? If so, they are indicating their own discomfort at your closeness. The right thing to do will be for you not to advance any further, or even to take a step back to show you respect their boundary.

There are a number of ways in which people register their discomfort or fear of having their personal space infringed. Look out for some of the following essential clues including the other person turning sideways to you, avoiding eye contact, keeping their responses brief, their lack of distinct speech, standing straighter and folding their arms across their chest, nervously flicking their hair or constantly touching of their face, or constant body movement or regular changing of their weight from one foot to the other.

Recognizing these cues becomes a challenge because everyone has their one, unique way of showing their discomfort when their boundaries are crossed. The secret of good communication and empathy is to be able to interpret these signs and to abide by the request they signal.

Seek Permission

Some people are unable to give consistent non-verbal clues about their boundaries. This lack of action may be due to the fact that they have no firm boundaries, or they don't understand the importance of guarding their personal space. They may not have been taught the importance of boundaries or may not have had a good example to follow.

When the signals someone sends out are confusing, it may be best to ask if you make the person feel uncomfortable and if so, would they prefer that you step back, or even leave the conversation. It is also a good gesture to ask if you may hold their hand or if a hug is acceptable before you rush in to grab the person. Most people respond well to being treated with sensitivity and care. By asking if you are infringing their boundaries, you place yourself in a nonaggressive, safe, and respectful light that others will appreciate and that will invoke a positive response.

Successful Ways in Which to Show Respect

Boundaries not only protect us from other people, they also strengthen our relationships and help us develop strong bonds with those we love and respect. Our intuition acts as an early warning for potentially harmful interactions. Often, we may ignore these important signals because we believe we are being unreasonable, unfair in our assessment of someone, or simply silly.

Intuition is a deeply seated sense, buried in your subconscious mind. It has the power to interpret danger and to give you notice to withdraw as quickly as possible. Some refer to this sensation as your sixth sense. Whatever term you use to identify this feeling, it is essential to take heed when you feel that sense of unease.

No relationship is ever truly one-sided. Successful relationships rely on communication, energy, and effort. The bond between people can be substantially strengthened when parties know, recognize, and understand each other's limits. Your actions inadvertently impact other people and affect how they feel about you and how they interact with you.

The importance of recognizing the boundaries other people have set up is of paramount importance to your positive, continued relationship. Ignoring these boundaries will inevitably lead to the destruction of the friendship or relationship.

Setting boundaries is not simply about building barriers around yourself. Nor does it entail fencing yourself in and others out. Boundaries work for each person to ensure there are limits to your patience, kindness, time, and goodwill. When these boundaries are understood by those you love and spend time with, the rules for committed, positive, and constructive interaction are clear to everyone who participates in the relationship. For each person, boundaries help them discover what makes them happiest, brings them peace and a sense of belonging and security.

Sometimes, there are occasions when you choose to say "no" or feel it is in your best interest to walk away from a situation. Don't beat yourself up about these decisions. Instead, use them as an opportunity to reassess the situation, understand what is happening, and then gather your energy to re-group.

It's important to realize your self-worth. Setting boundaries allows you opportunities to take care of your own needs before those of others. Developing boundaries takes a great deal of practice as our subconscious often gets in the way, telling us to step up for others first. Admirable though selfless acts are, the rewards of learning to take care of your own needs first outweigh any egotistic fantasies you have from providing service to others.

However, although it's important to acknowledge that you are the most important entity in your life, you should be mindful of the fact that each person feels the same about themselves, also. Being in charge of your life and comfortable to stand by your values means you are fully aware of the same expectations of others.

Stay on the Alert

Improving your self-awareness in every situation in which you find yourself can help you predict success or avoid potential disaster. Your personal boundaries create a barrier for your protection. When you learn to listen to your secret voice and obey its messages, you become more attuned to your inner being. With this, your self-confidence improves, and you can make decisions to satisfy your needs and wants first. Making a conscious decision to listen to your inner voice and prioritize yourself is a crucial step that's needed to help you begin the practice of setting boundaries. When this understanding develops, you are in a great position to divert your energy for activities and interests that bring you joy, happiness, and a sense of accomplishment.

Respecting the boundaries of others is paramount to your success in any relationship, be it formal, social or within your family. When your own boundaries are in place, you automatically become more intuitively aware of other people's boundaries. This knowledge leads to greater mutual respect, understanding, and trust.

Your boundaries may make you appealing to some people because they feel safe and secure around you. These barriers also help you to realize that you don't have to humor everyone all the time. By having your boundaries in place, these allow you the freedom to extend your goodwill when it is suitable to do so, while recognizing the importance of the other person's boundaries as well as their efforts to please you.

Setting good personal boundaries makes it possible for you to develop a firm framework in which to not only care for your own needs, but to also successfully support others in need of your care. Good boundaries ensure you feel safe and secure. Hence, you have the energy and ability to feel happy, content, and positive.

When you have positive vibes, the world around you will also respond positively.

Your Boundaries Grow with You

When you were a child, you may have experienced the excitement and enthusiasm of new discoveries such as a trickle of water over a fluted rock in the forest. Or, perhaps an interesting multi-legged mini creature hiding beneath a piece of fallen timber. There was novelty and treasure in every new revelation. As we age and mature, we may exhibit less enthusiasm for new discoveries and attempt to hide our interest in life in case our feelings are judged for something inane and childish.

At times, we may feel that our boundaries become burdensome, and we may find it challenging to maintain them. This is a sign that we need to look inward in order to try to make sense of ourselves and our lives. By studying our innermost self and understanding the reasons for our boundaries, we attain a higher level of self-knowledge that lends our lives to authenticity and value.

Understanding Your Past

Learning to look deep into your psyche and examine memories that are hurtful or loving and tender, takes courage. Your memories were formed by past events over which you may or may not have had much control over. These memories are seared into your subconscious from where they influence all that you now say, think, and do.

The boundaries that you have established are often founded on experiences, which can sometimes be emotionally draining, fettering your progress and future achievements. The past is thus always present. It is how you allow it to influence your current life that holds the key to your success or failure to interact with other people and live your best life.

When it comes to confronting your own memories, by recognizing the courage it takes to face the past and to then forgive yourself for things you did or failed to do, you are also in a better, more positive position to build new, stronger boundaries.

Violating other people's boundaries here will be ignoring the personal memories that they hold dear. Thus, disrespectful passive-aggressive responses that include interrupting people when they share their precious memories or gossiping about these memories to others is an infringement of their boundaries, as those memories make up who they are. So, just as your memories have played an important role in shaping who you are as an individual today, be mindful that you should also be respecting other people's memories for this very same reason.

During your inner exploration of your memories, you may inadvertently discover a great deal of pain and heartache that you have been unable to let go of. Every sad and hurtful occasion can often be recollected far quicker than the happier events. It is usually these negative memories that drive one's life story.

Being human may lead you to make assumptions about certain situations and other people. For the sake of others, try to take a step back and see their past as objectively as you can in order to allow yourself to understand how that person came to be. While it may be helpful to learn about or consider their past to understand how they developed into the person that they are, try to not allow their history to dictate your current perception of them, and try to see them purely for the person that they are today. This will help you to understand someone else's perspective without passing unnecessary and unfair judgement.

Developing a sense of curiosity will encourage you to look into the life and actions of others whom you are interacting with so that you do not assume their past will also represent their future. Just as we should avoid making assumptions and conclusions about other people based on their past experiences, we must also do the same for ourselves. If we make an effort to revisit our memories and past events stored in our subconscious mind, we may be able to draw fresh conclusions about these past events which may provide us with greater clarity, and perhaps a truer picture of the progression of our own self-development and identity.

Angela and Gary

Angela had been married to her husband Gary for over 30 years. Gary, who was seriously overweight often used emotional blackmail to keep his wife at home with him because he was embarrassed about going out in public. Over the years, Angela became reliant on Gary for her income as his wealthy family had left him enough funds on which to live out his life in relative comfort.

After many years of Angela catering to Gary's needs, with Gary frequently coercing her into submission, things reached a head when Gary suffered a massive heart attack. Gary had to spend weeks at the hospital, and Angela found that she would be home alone for the first time in years. She spent the days doing whatever she pleased as she was no longer required to tend to Gary's needs anymore.

During the days alone, she finally came to realize how unhappy she had been in the relationship. The boundaries that she had set earlier in the marriage had all but disappeared, and she realized that she had become nothing more than a prisoner in her own home. She found herself trying to pinpoint the moment when things changed, or when Greg had overstepped the line. The memories that flooded her made her weep from how weak she had been. She couldn't help but think that her inaction in her situation meant that she was solely responsible for her current predicament.

But she was determined to make a change now.

When Gary came home, Angela found the voice that she needed to give Gary her ultimatum. She would find herself a job and she would claim back her autonomy! Angela still loved Gary, but if he could not respect her newfound boundaries, she would pack her bags and leave.

Gary had never seen Angela so determined. He found that he had little choice but to respect her decision, as she had drawn a very clear line of what was no longer acceptable to her.

Angela would later find work at the local market, where she was able to pick up new skills and meet new people. She had never felt happier in her life.

A Final Word

Though everyday boundaries can be seen as the invisible lines that seemingly separate you from others, these lines have huge value not only for your safety, but also for your well-being, health, and happiness. In order for boundaries to be successful, they require constant readjustment and emphasis. Vigilance is required, especially when you experience pushback from people who disagree with your boundaries or feel the need to test the strength and resilience of your barriers.

Boundaries encourage predictability. They help to keep you feeling secure, manage self-care, and enable you to make healthy, sensible choices. Your boundaries are also closely linked to your instincts, needs, values, and rights. Maintaining sound, flexible boundaries is key to learning to trust yourself, whilst also relying on your intuition as a tool to ensure your own safety and wellbeing.

Without personal boundaries in place, you will find that you are more likely to waste your emotional energy on resentment, fear, or mental anguish.

The Value of Boundaries in Your Life

The greatest benefit of having solid boundaries is that they set a precedent for you not to have to do anything you don't want to do. The wonderful thing is that you are free to choose to participate in events that lift your spirits, freely walk and talk with whomever you feel happy to spend time with, all without feeling any of the guilt that others may expect you to feel.

Well-designed boundaries empower you and help you conserve valuable energy by having the courage to turn down extra tasks and avoid unwanted added responsibilities, while also allowing you to set time aside for much-needed self-care. These boundaries will also afford you the opportunity to spend time with those who matter most to you.

You may have come to believe that boundaries will curtail your freedom to grow and prosper. I'm sure now you know that it is in fact the opposite – boundaries allow you the space to grow and fill your life with positive people, pleasurable activities, and with an abundant opportunity for health, wealth, and happiness.

Boundaries encourage you to view your life in a more realistic and objective way, thus affording you the chance to make changes to your group of friends, your commitments, and your lifestyle. Once you have assessed your life in terms of your values and go ahead in deciding on, or adjusting your existing boundaries, I can assure that you will see a paradigm shift in your perspective and you will be grateful that you have drawn that line in the first place.

Remember, good, solid personal boundaries should boost your self-esteem, reinforce your values, and encourage your growth in all aspects of life. It should allow you the opportunity to spread your wings to discover your own true personal happiness and health.

Don't let others decide on how you live your life, anymore. You are in control. Always remember that this life is for you to live – so live it happily and healthily, as you deserve.

Resources

Castrillon, Caroline. "10 Ways To Set Healthy Boundaries At Work." *Forbes*, www.forbes.com/sites/carolinecastrillon/2019/07/18/10-ways-to-set-healthy-boundaries-at-work/#4f70eb3e7497.

Chesak, Jennifer. "The No BS Guide to Protecting Your Emotional Space." *Healthline*, Healthline Media, 10 Dec. 2018, www.healthline.com/health/mental-health/set-boundaries.

Cikanavičius, Darius. "An Introduction To Boundaries and Why We Need Them." *Psych Central.com*, 24 Sept. 2018, https://blogs.psychcentral.com/psychology-self/2018/09/intro-healthy-boundaries/.

Contessa, Career. "How to Establish Healthy Boundaries at Work." *Career Contessa*, 3 Feb. 2020, www.careercontessa.com/advice/healthy-boundaries-at-work/.

Djunga, Heather. "10 Ways To Set Healthy Boundaries With Children." *Moms*, 3 Oct. 2019, www.moms.com/healthy-boundaries-children-parents/.

Fernandez, Celia. "10 Celebrities on the Importance of Setting Boundaries." *Oprah Magazine*, 21 Nov. 2018, www.oprahmag.com/life/relationships-love/g23323893/celebrity-setting-boundaries-quotes/.

Forbes, Bo. "A Sequence + Meditation for Setting Healthy Boundaries." *Yoga Journal*, 13 June 2016, www.yogajournal.com/practice/sequence-meditation-setting-healthy-boundaries

Houlis, Annamarie. "5 Things Successful People Do When Setting Boundaries at Work." *Fairygodboss.com*, https://fairygodboss.com/career-topics/setting-boundaries-at-work.

Kabir, Homaira. "When Was the Last Time You Truly Examined Your Life?" *Goodnet*, 20 July 2016, www.goodnet.org/articles/when-was-last-time-you-truly-examined-your-life.

Manktelow, James, and Rachel Thompson. "What Are Your Values?: – Deciding What's Most Important in Life." *www.Mindtools.com*, www.mindtools.com/pages/article/newTED_85.htm#:~:text=Defining%20Your%20Values.

Mann, Mirele. "19 Stellar Pieces of Advice from 19 CEOs." *Goodnet*, 2 Oct. 2015, http://goodnet.org/articles/19-stellar-pieces-advice-from-19-ceos.

Manson, M. (2013, January 14). *The Guide to Strong Relationships*. https://markmanson.net/boundaries.

Maros, Michelle. "The Importance of Setting Boundaries." *Peaceful Mind Peaceful Life*, 1 Oct. 2017, http://peacefulmindpeacefullife.org/importance-setting-boundaries/.

Martin, Sharon. "Setting Boundaries with Yourself: An Essential Form of Self-Care." *Live Well with Sharon Martin*, 6 Aug. 2019, https://livewellwithsharonmartin.com/setting-boundaries-with-yourself/.

Mcleod, Saul. "Attachment Theory." *Simplypsychology.Org*, Simply Psychology, 5 Feb. 2008, www.simplypsychology.org/attachment.html.

Nazish, Noma. "Practicing Self-Care Is Important: 10 Easy Habits To Get You Started." *Forbes*, 19 Sept. 2017, www.forbes.com/sites/payout/2017/09/19/practicing-self-care-is-important-10-easy-habits-to-get-you-started/#419e893d283a.

Nouri, Cameron. "6 Effects of Poor Employee communication." *Pingboard*, 27 June

2019, http://pingboard.com/blog/6-effects-poor-employee-communication/.

O'Mara, Lori. "9 Ways to Set Boundaries with Difficult Family Members." *Cope Better*, 15 Oct. 2016, www.copebetter.com/9-ways-set-boundaries-difficult-family-members/.

Radin, Sara. "How to Create Boundaries With a Toxic Family Member." *Allure*, 13 Nov. 2019, www.allure.com/story/toxic-family-how-create-boundaries.

Rogers, Kali. "Setting Boundaries Benefits by a Life Coach." *Blush Life Coaching*, 17 Oct. 2019, https://joinblush.com/9-benefits-of-setting-boundaries/.

Sanchez, A. (2017, February 15). *Setting Boundaries in a Relationship*. Break the Cycle. https://www.breakthecycle.org/blog/setting-boundaries-relationship#:~:text=Establishing%20healthy%20boundaries%20in%20a.

Scott, Elizabeth. "The Importance of Self-Care for Health and Stress Management." *Verywell Mind*, Verywell mind, 10 Nov. 2019, www.verywellmind.com/importance-of-self-care-for-health-stress-management-3144704.

Selva, Jaoquin. "How to Set Healthy Boundaries: 10 Examples + PDF Worksheets." PositivePsychology.com, 5 Jan. 2018, http://positivepsychology.com/great-self-care-setting-healthy-boundaries/.

Song, Michelle. "Healthy Boundaries: Setting and Respecting Them." *Student Services*, 19 Aug. 2019, https://students.ubc.ca/ubclife/healthy-boundaries-setting-respecting-them.

Taberner, Kathy, and Kirsten Siggens. "Setting Boundaries & Why You Need Them." *Institute Of Curiosity*, 28 Jan. 2018, www.instituteofcuriosity.com/boundaries-why-you-need-them/

Tartakovsky, Margarita (a). "7 Tips for Setting Boundaries At Work." *World of Psychology*, 8 July 2018, https://psychcentral.com/blog/7-tips-for-setting-boundaries-at-work/.

Tartakovsky, M (b). (2018, July 08). 6 Vital Facts About Boundaries. https://psychcentral.com/blog/6-vital-facts-about-boundaries/.

van de Geyn, Lisa. "How to Deal with Your Preschooler's Copycat Behaviour." *www.Todaysparent.com*, 15 Jan. 2018, www.todaysparent.com/kids/copycat-kids-why-they-do-it/#:~:text=%E2%80%9CChildren%20copy%.

Weiss, Suzannah. "How To Set Boundaries With Your Family, According To A Life Coach." *Bustle*, 31 Mar. 2019, www.bustle.com/p/how-to-set-boundaries-with-your-family-according-to-a-life-coach-16980926.

Wojno, Rebecca. "6 Unexpected Benefits of Setting Clear Boundaries." *Goodnet*, 16 Dec. 2016, www.goodnet.org/articles/6-unexpected-benefits-setting-clear-boundaries.

Manufactured by Amazon.ca
Bolton, ON